CONOCIMIENTOS
PRESS

HOME, WHERE MEMORIES WAIT TO BE REMEMBERED

~ A TESTIMONIO ~
GROWING UP ON SAN ANTONIO'S WESTSIDE

Teresa Villarreal Rodriguez

CONOCIMIENTOS
PRESS

PUBLISHED BY CONOCIMIENTOS PRESS, LLC
SAN ANTONIO, TEXAS

ISBN: 978-1-7351210-5-5

CONOCIMIENTOSPRESSLLC.COM

To friends and family who contributed
to making me the person I became, particularly
my now departed husband of fifty-years,
Leonard E. Rodriguez. To *mi gente de San Antonio,*
especially those of you from the Westside—
thank you for the memories. Most of all, thanks
to my children Leonard and Lauren, family
and friends for believing in me and encouraging
me to write—here are my stories to honor
your presence in my life.

~ STORIES ~

TERESA'S BIOLOGICAL PARENTS—
JUANITA AND SANTOS VILLARREAL

BUILDING COMMUNITY, MAKING FAMILY FROM SCRATCH

Here's the thing. When I recall those growing up years with my blended family in our small, humble home on San Antonio's Westside, the poorest section in town, I mostly recall happy times. Even though we experienced hard times, romanticizing those years allows me to remember the good times and bury the bad. As I ran into people who were raised in the area, they also shared recollections of the time in our beloved neighborhood as the best years of their lives. For a lifetime, I've been trying to figure out why we shared these rosy common feelings despite growing up mired in poverty.

I started writing these stories more years ago than I care to admit. I was in my early 40's when I began to record them. The first one was about my paternal grandmother, Mama Tere, who came to live with us when our mother, Juanita, died of tuberculosis at the age of thirty-seven. I was a mere four months old, and my siblings were two, four, eight, and ten. My father, Santos, had two successful businesses at the time and had a nervous breakdown, losing his life's work.

Shortly after that tragic loss and a few months after my mother's death, my father sought Mama Tere's help and also asked his only sister, Ruby, if she and her family could move in until he came up with a better plan. A couple of weeks after that request,

Aunt Ruby and her husband Edmundo and their daughter Yolanda came to live with us.

That's the way this blended family of mine came to be—three separate families and three generations living in a small three-bedroom, one bath house. We navigated living with others who had distinct personalities, moods, and insecurities. In grace and with enduring love, we would learn to contend with disappointment.

Despite the adjustments we made, life with Mama Tere remained mysterious, unconventional, and puzzling. As a well-known Curandera, she used her extensive knowledge of plants, herbs, roots, and tree barks to treat people's various ailments with teas and ointment she prepared. To alleviate their pain she also gave deep tissue massages with her gifted hands. With ancient native rituals she cured people of *susto* and treated anxiety, depression, stress, and fear. During demon-filled storms, she would step outside into the drenching rain to *cortar las nubes* with prayer, a wooden cross, and a knife wrapped in white linen. Still a devout Catholic, she began and ended each day with prayer, kneeling before her altar overflowing with all her favorite saints and photos of family, living and deceased. She never hesitated to use both her traditional teachings and religious beliefs for the good of the people.

Our Tía Ruby (who became Mama Ruben to me) kept our family axis perfectly balanced. She was the peacekeeper between the children and especially with her mother, Mama Tere, and her husband, Papa Mundo, since there was consistently a tension between them. *Mama era una Santa.* Mama Ruben cooked, sewed our clothes, and performed miracles with Papa Mundo's paycheck and the money sent by my father, Santos. She celebrated our birthdays and special holidays, and kept the memory of Juanita, our mother, present.

SANTOS AND PAUL, WITH FATHER SANTOS SR.

Our Tío Mundo (Papa Mundo to me) was a life force. He was rough, loud, short fused, and a ball of fire. I learned to disappear when he was in a bad mood; it was as if he had an on-and-off switch without control. He worked the night shift at Kelly Air Force Base and after he got home and slept a while, he was in constant motion. He would jump in his car and go to the store to buy whatever was on special—like cans of green beans or peas—even though we already had a dozen or two in our pantry. Other times, he would go visit friends or his only sister who never married and who lived nearby. Papa Mundo was a hard worker. Besides his full-time job, he also worked part time at the mailroom of the Express-News. He found weekend jobs for my two oldest brothers and several of their friends to keep them out of trouble.

The only person that could keep him in line was Mama Ruben. Whenever she'd had enough, she would start raging. He would become as gentle as a lamb and tell her, "*Ya, Ruby. Ya.*" At *times* he was fun, comical, and generous. He often found a way to take us and an extra kid or two to the circus and to every air show in town. Life could be treacherous in our neighborhood, but most people knew they had better not mess with Mundo's kids or they would be sorry.

I grew up in San Antonio's Westside during the '50s and '60s. It was a poor, segregated Mexican American side of town with a sprinkling of (mostly) Catholic Germans and Polish families who decided to stay after the white flight to the Northside took place sometimes in the late 50s and early 60s. For most of the people living outside this *vecindario*, the Westside was forgotten, feared, misunderstood, vilified, and declared off-limits. Unbeknownst to outsiders, ours was an interconnected community where people knew one another, helped each other, and neighbors watched over children playing freely throughout the neighborhood.

The Westside was a neighborhood where people struggled to put food on their table, yet life was boisterous and vibrant. Women dressed in black if in mourning or otherwise in loud colors such as enchilada red, lime green, mango orange, lemon yellow, and aqua blue. Simple meals were prepared, and our salivary glands exploded on our return home from school in the later afternoon as we inhaled mouthwatering aromas that drifted out of small, cramped kitchens where *tomates* and *chiles* sizzled on red-hot grills as perfectly round homemade tortillas baked on a cast iron comal.

This place where I grew up was a typical Mexican American neighborhood, like others throughout the country, bursting with a rich and endearing culture. It was a place where families gathered to make *piñatas* for special occasions, *cascarones* for Easter, and assembled homemade kites with sticks, newspaper, and home-made glue. We participated in traditions of *bolo*, *tamaladas*, Christmas *posadas*, and the *Tres Reyes* re-enactments.

Make no mistake, this was not Mr. Roger's neighborhood. Life was hard and people suffered the consequences of poverty—drugs, crime, family violence, teenage pregnancy, depression, and suicide. And, unfortunately, many families lacked access to physical and mental health services and transportation while living with food insecurity. The only government assistance to be had was the Surplus Commodities program which was very limited.

My side of town was not about this one thing or the other. It was everything. It was a unified neighborhood where people who had little still found a way to share their generosity and take care of one another. Most adults stepped up and took care of their family, and most children grew up in a safe and simple environment where they felt protected and respected. Even though we lacked material possessions, we had love—the thing that mattered most.

For over thirty years I've written stories about my immediate family, our neighborhood, and our rich culture, traditions, rituals, and the values that have persisted for hundreds of years. These are values that are sadly vanishing for our descendants and our communities. There have been many times when I've stored away my writings with finality, telling myself that I had written enough stories to gift my children, grandchildren, and extended family with a history of how we grew up. But something or someone prods me to continue writing. Perhaps it has been my desire to know more about my parents' history that has pushed me to leave a written record about mine, or maybe, just maybe, it has been my Mama Tere all along, whispering in my ear to write it all down. Nonetheless, I am compelled to write so that future generations become inspired to unearth their roots, to reclaim their culture, and hopefully to create a sense of belonging no matter where the world takes them.

MAMA TERE AND YOLANDA

MEXICO LINDO
Y QUERIDO

When Teresa Cuellar Villarreal left to *El Norte* she only told her father, mother, and Sol—an Indian Mexican woman who had been part of her family as far back as she could remember. She loved her as deeply as she loved her parents, or perhaps more. Teresa often said that Sol taught her everything she knew about plants, herbs, roots, and barks which she used to treat various maladies. She also learned much about the afterlife, where many of Sol's people now rested.

Soon after the Mexican Revolution of 1910 exploded, Teresa's husband, Santos Villarreal, and his older brother, Virgilio, joined General Francisco "Pancho" Villa to fight against the corrupt Porfirio Diaz—a dictator who had controlled Mexico for thirty years. While fighting in Northern Mexico Santos and Virgilio were wounded, and, when word of their injuries reached their families, Teresa and her sister-in-law boarded the first train toward Chihuahua to go tend to their men and bring them home. Santos' injury was grave and to care for him Teresa stayed in Chihuahua for several months. At the camp they lived in, she tended wounded fighters and assisted with the cooking. As soon as the doctor released Santos to travel, they finally returned to the family's ranch. Months later, Santos died. Teresa

changed course to follow through with a plan she had hatched
when her husband rode off with Pancho Villa. She understood that,
with the death of her husband, her son who was twelve years old
would be conscripted into any one of the many *ista* forces: *Villista*,
Federalista, *Zapatista*, and *Carrancista*. She was bound to say, "*Perdí
a mi marido a la revolución, y mis hijos perdieron a su padre, pero yo
no iba a perder mi hijo.* I lost my husband, and my children lost their
father to the revolution, and I wasn't going to lose my son."

Time was running out for her. It was only a matter of time
before government troops or revolutionaries rode to the ranch for
food, animals, and God forbid, her only son, and the women.

Several days after Santos' funeral, Teresa instructed Sol to
load one of the wagons full of maíz and vegetables because she
and her children would be leaving that night. Dressed as ordinary
campesinos with several layers of clothes to keep them warm,
Lupe, a trusted old ranch hand, steered the wagon and prayed
they wouldn't run into military troops or roving bands of thieves.
After one long night on the beaten path, they reached the Mexico-
Texas border where Teresa and her children boarded a train to
San Antonio. From there, they made their way to Geronimo, Texas,
outside Seguin, where they lived with cousins who had also fled
Mexico because of the Revolution. To pay for their expenses, Teresa
and her children picked cotton until they moved to San Antonio.

In San Antonio, Teresa supported her family by sewing for the
wealthy. In time she decided to use the money she brought with
her across the border to open a restaurant she called Venice which
was located at the corner of Guadalupe and Zarzamora Streets.
Seven days a week she and her children worked long hours and built
a prosperous business. Later, and with much success, the family

inaugurated a larger restaurant and bakery named *El Progreso Café* on Guadalupe Street.

Teresa, the *abuela* who would become my Mama Tere, recognized that her sacrifice to leave *Mexico lindo y querido*, her birth family, and her way of life had been well worth the peace of mind and safety she found for her children and herself. She was willing to leave everything behind except for her rich culture, traditions, and rituals which she was determined to pass on to future generations. She would have never imagined the tragedy that awaited them.

ASÍ HICIMOS FAMILIA

The house was quiet that day. Everyone was out except for Mama Ruben, grandmother, and me. I longed to know how I came to live with my aunt and uncle. For this reason, I asked them about our family constitution. This is what I heard to the best of my recollection.

Mama Ruben

"Two weeks after you were born, your father Santos called. He asked if I could pick you up. To care for you until your mother Juanita felt better. '*Una o dos semanas,*' he said—just two weeks! That same day, Edmundo and I went for you. With much concern, your mother locked eyes with me, and said, '*Te la encargo. Cuídala mucho.*' I replied, '*Con mi vida.* With my life.'"

When we got home, Edmundo set up the small cradle I had kept after Yolanda was born, never giving up hope that we would have more children. That day, when Yolanda walked in from school, she looked at the cradle, ran up to it, and saw you sleeping there. Her eyes grew perfectly round like saucers and her joyous smile filled the room. The three of us leaned over the crib and stared at you. We couldn't

TERESA AND YOLANDA

believe what we were seeing, each one of us lost in our own thoughts. "No. No estábamos culecas. No. No. Estábamos trastornadas contigo."

Mama Ruben said she never stopped asking *la Virgen de Guadalupe* to intercede on her behalf to have more children. But it didn't happen.

"Then you came. *Hija, fuiste un milagro.* Child, you were a miracle. But I never stopped praying that your mother would get well. Never! You needed your mother, and I wanted to take you home where you belonged. I wanted the day to come when I could place you in your mother's arms.

"A few months after you'd been with us, your father called. He told me that Juanita wanted to talk to me—she must've not been doing well.

"When I arrived, Juanita looked into my eyes and said, '*Te quiero pedir algo. Cuídame a mis hijos,* please take care of my children.' Once again, I reassured her with my words: '*Con mi vida. Te lo juro.'*

"*Dios es muy grande.* God is great. I'd been praying for at least another child, but God had a greater plan. He sent me two additional daughters, and three sons, and each one of you has been a blessing."

Mama Tere

"*Cuando tu Mama pidió hablar con Rubensita me quede en casa con Yolanda y contigo. Me quede preocupada. Tu Mama ya tenia días que estaba agonizando. Sufriendo demasiado. Yo estaba preparando la cena cuando la casa trono fuerte. En ese momento supe que tu madre había muerto; que su espíritu había salido de su cuerpo. Mi corazón se puso muy triste y pensé en tu padre Santos y todos ustedes: Santos Junior, Pablo, Juanita, Jesús, y tu, Teresita, y tambien pensé en tu otra abuela, Dolores y tu tío Jesús.*

"*¡Que tristeza! ¡Que dolor tan profundo!*"

"When your mother asked to speak to Rubensita, I remained at home with Yolanda and you. I was concerned. It'd been days since your mother had been agonizing. Suffering. I was preparing dinner when the house made a strong, thundering sound. It was at that moment that I knew your mother had passed; her spirit had left her body. My heart was filled with sadness, and I thought of your father Santos and all of you: Santos Junior, Polo, Janie, Jesse, and you, Teresita, and I also thought about your other grandmother, Dolores, and your uncle Jesse.

"What deep sadness! What intense pain!"

Despite our difficulties, my new family made life magical and interesting. I would learn so much from them.

PAPA MUNDO AND MAMA RUBEN

MAMA TERE, SLAYER OF STORMS

"Ocurre durante los entremedios," my grandmother Mama Tere said of those in-between days no longer bound to the passing season or quite anchored to the incoming one, when demons are released and emerge to create all kinds of chaos. They brought powerful storms that ravaged communities and filled people with despair. By this time, I had learned that spirit people have special authority to fight and defeat evil.

Mama Tere and I were in the backyard sorting plants and herbs used for cooking, teas, and poultices used for healing. We were busy digging for bulbs, pulling dead vegetation, and rearranging weathered stones that separated one group of plants from the other when I sensed a slight charge in the air. I stopped working and glanced over at my grandmother, but she didn't react. "Surely if I noticed this change, she had too," I thought. But she continued with the chores at hand, deciding which plants, herbs, and bulbs to discard or store for the following season.

Sometime later, I heard the faintest sound of wind gently rustling the treetops and sweeping quietly from tree to tree in a continuous embrace, whispering intimacies of love. I inhaled that earthy scent of wet dirt and clay produced by rain. Again, I looked over at Mama Tere, but she kept up with the weeding, digging, and re-claiming. A few minutes later, my grandmother slowly rose to her feet and began to move towards the back door. As she started to climb the three wooden steps to go inside, she looked over her shoulder and said, "*Ya llego la tempestad hija. Metete.*" The storm had arrived. I hurried inside as cold, heavy raindrops pummeled my head and back.

When we went to bed that evening—me in my twin bed and my grandmother in hers—I could hear rain drumming our tin roof. Then, before I slept, I watched my grandmother kneel before the altar to begin her nightly prayers to *La Virgen de Guadalupe* and all her saints. The soft murmur of her rhythmic voice and the mesmerizing dancing lights on the ceiling, produced by the flicker of her altar's devotional candle, lulled me to sleep.

The storm gathered substantial strength and it rained most of the night. Intermittently, I woke to the sound of strong wind and rain. At times it sounded like monsters were scratching at our roof and wailing, determined to find an entry point. Sometime during the storm, I awoke and noticed Mama Tere's now empty bed. Startled, I jumped and went to look for her, but I only found my two sisters in their room, my parents in theirs, and my two brothers asleep on the L-shaped sofa in the living room.

"Where is my grandmother and why is everyone sleeping with this powerful howling storm," I wondered, cautiously opening the door to step out to the front porch. The storm had painted the night black, and I couldn't make out a thing. About to come back inside, I faintly heard her voice over the roaring wind. There, straining my eyes to see and my ears to hear, bolts of lightning danced in the sky and set alight the inky night, and I saw my grandmother standing on the sidewalk. I watched her lift the plain, wooden cross above her; she faced north, and then east, south, and then west, praying as she moved in a circular motion. Then she pulled out a knife wrapped in white cloth and pointed it towards the sky. She began to pray to *Santa Barbara Doncella*, asking her for protection from the treacherous storm. I strained to hear her prayer, but her words were made inaudible by ear-splitting thunder and the sounds of drenching rain.

Slowly, as if slicing a piece of a newly baked loaf of bread and making the sign of the cross, she began to cut the clouds with her knife. Deep in prayer, Mama Tere continued this ancient ritual over and over. The storm resisted, but my grandmother never wavered as two mighty forces met: one fighting for protection, the other for destruction. I cringed as lightning fell around her. I tried to run. To protect her. Instead, I froze in place and my legs felt heavy— as though cement had been poured inside me. I could tell my grandmother was tiring and beginning to lose ground, but she never retreated. The storm began to lose its grip. The clouds slipped away, seeking a new place to inflict their misdeeds. Now, feeling safe from the storm, I quietly returned to bed.

On schedule, I awoke at five o'clock in the morning to see my grandmother kneeling in prayer before her altar, but I soon fell back asleep. Sometime later, I awoke to the soft sounds of her *palote* as she rolled a tall stack of tortillas for our breakfast and school lunches. Life had returned to normal.

A few days later, we received our copy of *La Prensa*, San Antonio's Spanish English newspaper. That evening, my brother Santos read about the powerful storm that had slammed into San Antonio and caused widespread but minor flooding. The entire city, including the Westside which often flooded with these types of storms, had been spared when the storm had unexpectedly fallen apart. Santos lifted his eyes from the page commenting, "Boy, I never even heard the storm. Did anyone?" We all looked at one another but no one responded. I glanced at my grandmother's face which appeared to say, "*Pudo ser que alguien corto las nubes.* Perhaps someone cut the clouds."

LA CURANDERA

It was a busy week for Mama Tere. Several people came knocking at our door asking for *la curandera*. She came out to meet them. Adan, who looked like he was in his early thirties, had a stiff neck and an unbearable pain which traveled all the way down his shoulder. Whenever he wanted to move his neck to either side, he had no choice but to shift his entire body. He was concerned that he hadn't been able to work for several days, and if he didn't work then his family couldn't eat. Mama Tere told him to return later that day— there were things to prepare. As things went, besides being a healer, she was also a *sobadora* who gave deep tissue massages.

Pedro, another young man who came calling, explained that he had stomach cramps and had not been able to keep anything down for days. My grandmother quizzed him about his symptoms. She sent me to find certain dry herbs and roots. She mixed them together, wrapped them in a square piece of cheese cloth by tying the four corners together, and, with brewing instructions, handed it to Pedro. She told him to drink it twice a day for three days and return if he didn't improve.

Later that afternoon Adan returned and asked, "How much do you charge?" to which Mama Tere replied, "No charge."

He said, "No *tengo mucho dinero*, but I'll have money in two days, when I get paid."

"*No te preocupes*. Relax," Mama Tere said and invited him to come in. She told him to sit on an old, sturdy stool which she had retrieved from a corner of our living room. With a sweet-smelling cream she had prepared earlier that day, Mama Tere oiled her hands and warmed them over the gas stove. Then she massaged his neck, shoulder, and upper arm, pressing hard to find the knots. Adan moaned in pain, but she persisted until it vanished. When Mama Tere was done, she applied the remainder of the cream on his skin, wrapped a wet, hot towel on his neck and shoulder, and told him to close his eyes and relax until the towel cooled down. Before Adan left, Mama Tere gave him a cup of hot tea. When he finished drinking it, she sent him on his way and told him to come back if he needed another massage.

The third client, Armando, asked Mama Tere if she could help Junior, his twenty-one-year-old son, who was suffering with severe anxiety and depression. She asked him a few questions and then told him, "*Tráemelo el miércoles, jueves y viernes. ¿Puedes venir los tres días? Porque si no puedes, estas perdiendo tu tiempo y el mío.*" The man responded that he would bring his son three consecutive days, asking instead for Monday, Tuesday, and Wednesday. Mama Tere replied, "No. *Tiene que ser miércoles, jueves y viernes.* It had to be Wednesday, Thursday, and Friday." Armando agreed to bring his son as requested. Thus, her unpaid work continued.

I once asked Mama Tere why she didn't charge for her work; God knows we could've used the money. She then shared her wisdom with me. "*Si acepto dinero, mañana nada cambia, seguimos pobres. Quizás ellos no puedan comprar leche para su bebe, ni* pagar la luz y la leche se pudre, al igual que nuestro corazón. El universo no trabaja así, hija. Cuando uno hace mal, se paga. Quizás no inmediatamente, pero puede ser con hijos, nietos, o tal vez otros descendientes. En tiempo, todo mal se paga. Nunca seas la razón que cause sufrimiento a otra persona, porque lo vas a pagar."

Even though Mama Tere didn't charge for her services, people she treated stopped by our house with warm homemade tamales, plants, pan dulce, fresh eggs, and live chickens. And there were times when people left an envelope with money.

If someone showed up at our door asking Mama Tere to use her gift to place a curse on someone, she would immediately tell them she only worked to do good in the world and send them on their way. She never wanted to be like our in-law relative curandero. He was rich and owned multiple properties downtown and throughout San Antonio and adjoining towns. People were desperate to heal their sons, daughters and loved ones from disease, both physical and mental. With payments for treating their loved ones' health and well-being, the in-law tío built his house, got this land, squirreled money, and collected heirlooms as he acquired more and more wealth.

One day, I asked Mama Tere why she didn't send some of her customers to the curandero. She said, "Si les digo que vallan con él, es como si yo misma hubiera hecho un mal. No tengo nada que ver con eso."

When Wednesday evening came around, as it had been arranged, Armando brought his Junior to see Mama Tere. As her helper, I fetched the clean, starched, and ironed white sheets, found her plain wooden cross, lit a candle, burned a small amount of salvia, and brewed tea. When they arrived, Mama Tere asked Junior to lie on a makeshift bed, covered him with the sheet, and began her ritual.

Mama Tere often treated the family. When this happened for me, I felt a euphoric sense of comfort and protection—it was like being enveloped in a cocoon of peace and harmony that lasted for months. However, as she got older, I started to notice that when she did a cure for *susto*, she appeared physically, mentally, and spiritually depleted, and often entered a deep sleep. I conveyed to Mama Ruben what I observed, and Mama started to limit access to those who came asking for help with *susto*.

This was Mama Tere's work. Many people came for healing, protection, and hope. She treated joint and muscle pains, severe headaches, stomach ailments, anxiety, depression, and insomnia. I was her assistant and warmed towels, brewed teas, and mixed concoctions. As I watched and learned, I joined in prayer. I loved my life with Mama Tere. Even when my siblings had married and left home, I chose to stay in that small bedroom with her, surrounded by her beloved saints, lit candles, and yellowed photos of stern looking relatives in plain wooden frames hanging on the wall alongside Pope John Paul and President Kennedy. The scent of the incense and dried herbs, which oozed from her every pore, comforted me.

Right before dawn on one ordinary day, the stillness in the room, the absence of her prayers and the immobility of the *palote* rolling out tortillas for our breakfast called, then screamed, for me to wake up. WAKE up! Frightened, I jumped out of bed and rushed to check on Mama Tere. I found her semi-comatose and ran to wake my parents. My mother immediately called the doctor who sent them to Grace Lutheran Hospital, which was only three blocks away on Zarzamora Street.

After examining Mama Tere with glistening tears in his eyes, Dr. Pate walked over to us and said there was nothing more that could be done. Mama Ruben let out a loud, pain-filled cry, and he wrapped his arm around her.

Mama said, "*Pero doctor*, she was fine last night. She's never been sick. How can this be?"

He agreed, "You're right. She is very healthy, but she's plumb tuckered out." My grandmother unexpectedly died.

Over the span of many, many years, I contemplated Mara Tere's life. I began to understand this brave woman who had been offered a gift—to bring relief to the suffering—and had unquestionably accepted it. For me, her spiritual gift and treating people for *susto* led to the internalization of their anxiety, depression, and fear; the greater their suffering, the greater the toll on her physical and mental well-being. And for all we know, this might've brought her early death.

Mama Tere was fearless. With her young children, she escaped during the Mexican Revolution after her husband died of bullet wounds while fighting with Pancho Villa. In her desire to prevent her son from being conscripted she had fled to *el norte*—the United States—where she labored tirelessly picking cotton in Geronimo, Texas, to provide food and shelter for her family. An entrepreneur, she successfully ran two restaurants in the heart of San Antonio's Westside. Mama Tere also had a deep understanding of the medicinal properties of plants, herbs, barks, and roots. She used her knowledge to help those who came seeking help. A gifted *curandera* in San Antonio's Westside, Mama Tere had treated hundreds of people with a variety of plants and traditional rituals. Most of all, she was our grandmother, and, after our mother Juanita had died, Mama Tere had spent the rest of her life loving and nurturing us and being our primary educator. In her care, we found new ways of knowing and mysterious lessons would appear in our midst out of nowhere.

HOUSE
LIMPIA

A few weeks after Christmas and the New Year, Mama Tere made
her annual announcement: "*Hijas, prepárense, mañana vamos a
darle una buena limpia a la casa.*" It was not about *limpiadas* or the
cleaning we did at the beginning of Spring by washing widows and
curtains, dusting blinds, and scrubbing floors. No, this *limpia* was
much more transformative. These *limpias* were always performed
during the first month of the year to rid our home of *malos humores*,
bad spirits, bad omens, *malas suertes*, serious illnesses and life-
threatening diseases that might've snuck in during the year. We
began when Mama Ruben instructed us to open every window and
all the doors, every box, and all the drawers while telling us "Don't
forget the kitchen cabinets and the refrigerator and stove doors,"
and Yolanda reminded us, about "the medicine cabinet in the
bathroom and lift the toilet seat."

Thus, the *limpia* began. Mama handed Yolanda, Janie, and
me brooms and we swept, swept, swept—inside every closet,
underneath the bed, behind furniture, under tables and chests.
We swept. Swept everything out, out, out, tossing it out the doors,
with the intent of purging evils from our home. Once we finished

sweeping, we sealed the house by closing outside doors and windows. Empowered by prayer, burning salvia, and holy water, our grandmother and mother walked through every room. They sprinkled holy water everywhere and exited. Then, my sister Janie and me would close every drawer, every box, every cabinet, and every door. When we were done, we retired to our rooms to rest and contemplate on the ritual in which we had just participated. As for me, I followed my sisters to their room expecting them to tell me, "*Largate, escuincla.*" But they let me stay with them and I heard them talk about an upcoming house party at the Salas. They were known to have the best *pachangas* but that wasn't the best of it; they also talked about boys, clothes, and the latest hair styles. It was fun.

After a while, Mama Tere became the topic of the conversation. Yolanda asked, "Do you ever think about how — I don't know— Mama Tere is different?"

Without thinking, I piped in, "She's not different. She's like every other *abuela.*"

"No, she isn't," Janie retorted.

Yolanda continued, "Don't you ever think about the things she does, like the *limpia* today, *susto*, and how she goes outside with her cross and *cuchillo* and cuts the clouds?"

I said, "Yea, but all *abuelas* do that."

But Janie said, "No they don't. Look at all the plants she grows, including marihuana, for all her *remedios* and how they grow wild." She stopped for a while and added, "Who else has an orchard in their back yard?" We had plums, peaches, pears, figs, Chinese plums, blackberries, *granadas*, and two pecan trees.

We paused, and Yolanda started again. "Don't you think it's strange how she's always talking to *santitos*, like they're family?"

That made me think about the times she would turn St. Anthony's face to the wall or more drastically when she took the baby away from him for days. I knew Mama Tere would do this because she had something very important to ask of St. Anthony. It usually had to do with someone's health, but I wasn't going to tell my sister.

To bring the conversation to a positive end, I reminded my sisters that she and Mama Ruben planned many celebrations for us, our *tamaladas* or tamal-making parties, when we put to bed baby Jesus at midnight, *Día de los Reyes*, and Easter traditions. Yolanda nodded and said, "I don't think any of this is bad, I just think she's different."

I said, "Well, I think she's special, extremely special."

My sisters agreed and returned to their favorite subject—boys.

This was but one of the many magical experiences I had among the women in my family. However, there would be others.

GODPARENTS GILBERT AND STELLA CARREÑO, THEIR CHILDREN RENE AND ROSEMARY,
WITH YOLANDA, MAMA RUBEN, PAPA MUNDO, AND TERESITA

LA ACOSTADITA: BABY JESUS FINDS A HOME

The banging sounds of pots and pans and running water coming from the kitchen woke me up, and I jumped out of bed with the realization that today was Christmas Eve. In a flash I dressed and went to the kitchen to witness organized chaos. Mama Tere and Mama Ruben were bustling, busy as bees with our annual *tamalada*. My mother was rubbing spices on a *cabeza de puerco* — pig's head. Once Mama Tere finished, she wrapped it in foil paper and put it in the oven. This would be the meat in our *tamales*, to complement the bean and chicken ones. Huge red chile pods and pieces of chicken were boiling on the stove. When Mama Tere saw me, she said, "Ay que bueno que ya despertaste. Limpia estos frijoles." I sat down and began to clean a tall mound of pinto beans. When my sister Janie joined us, she began to peel a stack of fresh garlic.

While we were hard at work, my *Madrina* Estela and my cousin Rosemary walked in with a big bag of *pan dulce* — Mexican sweet bread — and four extra hands. *Madrina* immediately began to slice pickled jalapeños and fresh onions for the chicken and bean tamales. Rosemary and I got busy cleaning the *hojas* which had been soaking in a kitchen sink filled with water to make them pliable and ready for spreading the *masa*.

Throughout the day, a few neighbors visited and checked on our tamal making and asked if we needed help. Mama Tere thanked them and told them, "No." It was she who spread the masa unto the corn husk and *Madrina* stuffed them. Thus, we continued until the last tamal was assembled and *Madrina* and Rosemary went home to change.

That evening, before my cousin Rosemary returned, my brother Jesse and I sat in front of the tree and the *Nacimiento*. We stared and guessed what each one of us saw. We could play that game for hours. When relatives and friends arrived, people gathered in our kitchen and living-dining room to eat our piping hot *tamales*, rice, beans, dips, and other dishes. Some people stayed indoors. Others went outside.

At midnight, Mama Ruben announced the laying of Jesus. Mama Tere, as the eldest, carried Baby Jesus wrapped in a blanket and asked Stella and Gilbert Carreño, the *padrinos*, to step forward. The *padrinos* gifted Baby Jesus with a new outfit and Estella changed his clothes. Afterwards, we prayed and sang. Then, the *padrinos* held the Baby and asked everyone to get in line to kiss the Baby's forehead and come to receive a gift from Baby Jesus—a wrapped caramel and pecan candy. Right before the laying of baby in the manger, the *padrinos* rocked him and asked those who wanted to rock him to step up. A few came forward. *Madrina* then handed Baby Jesus to Mama Tere who laid the baby in the manger as we sang *Noche de Paz*. As I looked around our small, crowded living room, people smiled and some had tears in their eyes.

After our guests left, we began to open our gifts. Each of the children had three gifts under the Christmas tree—one was from our parents, another from Papa Santos, and one from the *padrinos* Estella and Gilbert. These were simple, inexpensive gifts, but we were happy and thankful to have received them.

When I look back to my childhood Christmases, I see my family and friends standing in front of the manger watching Mama Tere as she placed Baby Jesus on his bed. Grown men and woman prayed, sang, listened, and watched with tears streaming from their eyes as they enacted this old tradition. I am forever grateful for these deep-rooted feelings of longing and belonging. The Westside of San Antonio was a magical place. In the everyday of life, with its rituals and cultural practices, I could always find things to do and enjoy myself just being in our neighborhood.

A BIT OF DIRT
AND A PILE
OF ROCKS

It was not unusual for something to suddenly appear on my side of town, San Antonio's Westside. There was talk of Angels appearing, sometimes a ghost, and even the Devil.

Mama Tere often spoke about the time our Blessed Mother appeared to her when my sister Janie had whooping cough and a dangerously high fever. Mama Tere had vowed not to get off her knees until her *nietecita* or granddaughter was healed.

Papa Mundo never forgot the time the devil appeared to him in the form of a wild boar that chased him when he was young. Lucky for him, he was able to outrun the boar and, get home safely before his father found out he wasn't even there, much less asleep in bed.

Even our dog Scotty appeared without an explanation at our doorstep one crisp Autumn morning with many unwanted cats that lived under the house.

People also appeared.

But no one could explain my sister's friend, *Hercilia*, who reappeared six months after mysteriously vanishing. What perfect timing! It just so happened that her parents had recently adopted a beautiful bouncing baby boy.

And, what about that grand old stately looking house that was placed across the street from ours?

With his graveyard shift at Kelly Air Force Base, Papa Mundo had plenty of time to waste during the day. One week Papa Mundo watched the dismantling of the old, two-way bridge on Buena Vista Street just West of downtown; the same bridge that took us in and out of the Westside. Generally, staying away from home kept Papa Mundo out of trouble. Life with him could be a daily calamity. Such was the case one day Papa Mundo asked a driver for his load: "What are you going to do with such fine dirt?"

The driver responded, "Dump it."

Well, at that very minute, it occurred to Papa Mundo to ask, "Can you dump it in our back yard? It's a mere mile away, maybe even closer."

The truck driver jumped at the offer. Without giving Papa Mundo time to think this through, or change his mind, the driver hopped into his truck, motioning for him to hurry up so he could go dump his cargo. That afternoon when I got home from school, I wasn't the least surprised at what greeted me; two humongous piles of rock and dirt which took up our entire back yard. The mounds were at least seven feet tall and five feet wide. I was so excited to see those magical mini hills. I couldn't believe our good luck!

Not everyone was excited. Mama Ruben was *enrabiada*, angry like a volcano about to explode. She couldn't believe that Papa Mundo had been so, so, gullible as to have someone dump that worthless junk into our yard. Mama Ruben ranted and raved about another *desastre*.

"*Por Dios, Edmundo, ¿Te vieron la "P" en la frente?* Did they see the "S" for stupid on your forehead?" Her language was not out of the ordinary. Mama Ruben was one of two people in our family who got away invoking God's name in one breath, while cursing. Papa Mundo, who wasn't religious, had license to curse. My siblings and me were forbidden from using such foul language.

In his defense, Papa Mundo rationalized that it was good dirt; "Free — *gratis* Ruby, *gratis*," soothingly adding, "*Cálmate mi amor*. Relax, it'll be good for the yard." Mama wasn't having any of it; she was not about to *cálmate*.

For her, it was not only "No," but hell to the no! As for Mama Tere, she simply raised her eyebrows, slightly shook her head, and went to pick *chile piquín*, cautioning me to "get your butt out," with a look, as she instructed me to pick only red ones.

A few days later it rained all night. The next morning the dirt had settled at the bottom of the load and gigantic pieces of cement with protruding horns were exposed. When my brother Paul and I walked outside and saw the mess, I told him, "Look, it even has horns."

He replied, "They're not horns, dummy, it's re-bar." When Mama Ruben looked outside the back door, she almost croaked. Her anger began to boil over, and she started to rant and rave again, only louder. When I saw how mad she was, I jumped on my bike and took off. I had a feeling Papa Mundo wanted his own bike to jump on and flee, but he had to stay and face the music.

For the next several months, my siblings and me, and neighborhood friends spent all afternoon playing cowboys and Indians, and cops and robbers, or simply ran up and down those hills, climbing those jagged cement pieces. We loved it!

Mama Ruben complained incessantly until Papa Mundo hired a company to haul the mess. We were crushed! Afterward, Mama griped that he was throwing away money to remove his fine dirt.

After all, she could've used it to help the church purchase new nicely padded kneelers.

After our hills disappeared, my siblings and I spent most Saturday mornings removing rocks from the dirt. We hated it! However, Mama Tere built herself—with my help, of course—a small rock wall around her ample flower garden and Papa Mundo was finally able to spread the small mounds of good dirt in our back yard. He could finally make peace with Mama Ruben.

In defense of Papa Mundo, I believe 2601 West Durango is the only home on the Westside, or, in the city, that has a piece of San Antonio's history. Although that dirt cannot speak, I'm here to give testimony. White flight was not the sole reality of our *vecindad*. When *bolillos* moved into our side of town, they also became a part of our environment.

HOUSE RELOCATION

Perhaps it was the loud unrestrained nonstop laughter or the jubilant squealing of children's voices, or it could've been the rhythmic clapping growing into a crescendo that brought us out of our home, pushing and shoving one another to see what was going on. The whistling called me.

"Where is the whistling coming from?" I asked my brother Paul. It was not the sound produced when we pursed our lips into a perfect round circle. Rather, it was more like pushing out air that rolled off the tongue by stretching the corners of the mouth with two fingers. It was a high-pitched sound that caught everyone's attention. The kind of sound that only Papa Mundo and my sister Yolanda expertly made, always leaving me quite envious.

If there was ever a need to use that screeching whistle, it was the time we saw a large stately house sitting atop a trailer in the middle of the street, as if standing for attention. Soon, we joined our neighbors who were down the street near Lanier, our neighborhood high school. As the house began lumbering its way toward us, neighbors came out dragging their kitchen chairs to watch the relocation. This was shaping up to be a fabulous day.

When neighbors heard about the moving house, they packed up their kids along with snacks and drinks. Some brought brightly colored blankets and umbrellas and hunkered down in people's yards to watch. As the house slowly inched forward, people took only quick breaks. They would run inside, fix a few sandwiches or tacos, and quickly return, afraid to miss something—like, you know, the house sliding off the trailer.

As if guiding a crawling caterpillar, the trucker clumsily drove the house forward. Sometimes the house swayed from side to side, and I imagined a wide-hipped woman that danced a slow *cumbia*—a rhythm that everyone in the Westside danced, regardless of age.

People weren't the only ones caught up by the commotion. Dogs not roped to trees or tethered to a clothesline, such as most dogs in our neighborhood, barked at the tow truck until they wore themselves silly. When the truck came to a standstill, and often without warning, dogs did their business as near to it as they could. People shouted and clapped. Some teen *payasos* tied a long rope to the front bumper of the trailer and the other end to their bikes. When the truck started moving again, the clowns pretended to pull the truck and the onlookers whistled, cheered, and laughed.

Since the driver only spent part of the day working on the project, his work lasted two days and left our street blocked, which caused a huge inconvenience. No one ever expected to come face-to-face with a moving house, especially those turning on Durango Street or going East.

While the relocation took place, having a grand time the only one not entertained was Mama Tere. She was *recta*—all about rules, and law and order. No one complained but soon enough Mama Tere asked, "¿Dónde está la policía? Where are the cops?" However, someone had to call for them first, and no one would. The last thing we wanted to see was *la policía* in our neighborhood. The issue of "*tus papeles*" was bound to come up. Heaven knows many neighbors would've vanished, as if they had never existed.

The following day, neighborhood women—who were called endearments such as *gordas, reinas, prietas, güeras*—pleaded with their men to stay home. They wanted their honeys, sweethearts, kings, darlings, and babes to take a day off. A day off was a good thing. The men were ready to rest their weary bones, achy bodies, heavy hearts, and fogged minds. A day off would spare them from getting up early and allow them to ignore the rooster and his singing caca-doodle-doing morning call. A day off work would be like a holiday. They were rested, they would return to their slaughterhouses, sweat shops, field work, construction sites, restaurant kitchens, and landscaping jobs.

The men were not the only ones who needed rest. Women also needed a break from their chores—to not be responsible for feeding chickens and skeletal-looking dogs and cats that showed up at their doorsteps. In desperation, the women even wished for the freedom of not tending to sick children and aging parents.

The house relocation and trailer were a distraction from daily responsibilities and became a reason for people to stage a neighborhood parade. To begin with, people tied their home-made brightly colored paper mache flowers to the wheels and *papel picado* banners to the trailer. They also decorated their kids' bikes, wagons, tricycles and strollers, as well as elderly folks' walkers and wheelchairs.

Not to be left behind, some of the women put on their sexy sequined dresses. *Flamenco* dancers wore their sultry attires and *tacones*, while others donned their folkloric garb and dancing shoes.

Some babies were fitted into their faded baptismal gowns and little girls dressed up in their white or yellowed communion dresses. A few veterans of World War I and II wore their old military uniforms and some ROTC high schoolers wore their new ones—afterall we were in military city USA. Several young men threw on their zoot suits, and one or two dressed up in old, rented tuxedoes and graduation caps, along with gowns that had been forgotten or never returned.

In the Westside, a party without music is no party. So, six high school band members brought out their instruments: one drum, one tuba, three horns, and one flute. Two moonlighting *mariachis* joined with their guitars. People marched, rode, skipped, walked, skated, and danced down the street to a rendition of *El Rey*. Everyone sang and waved at the spectators, though most had joined the parade. Everyone waved to display their pride.

In their view, the women saw themselves as the Queens—wearing gowns that cost more than most people in the Westside make in a year, riding elaborate floats in San Antonio's Battle of the Flowers parade. The interruption of the house relocation allowed them to set aside their worries, broken hearts, sorrows, fears, second jobs, broken cars, and overdue bills in the heap of memory.

When the house finally arrived at its final resting place, no one even knew because adults and *borrachos* insisted on keeping the block alive. That day, neighbors continued to run into their homes to fetch pitchers of cold water, lemonade, Kool-Aid in all the primary colors, beer, and appetizers until the wee hours of the morning.

My friends and I were having such a grand time that we forgot about the house. The next morning, the was house sitting right smack in the middle of our treasured Alamo the vacant lot across the street from our home that had been named after the lone tree that stood guard over several generations of neighborhood baseball players, not the famous Alamo. Sadly, the *pinche* house now occupied home plate, first, and second base and had stolen our baseball field. Eventually we found another vacant lot for our games. We used the rocks and weeds from cleaning the field to fill the holes and make it usable.

We grew up and moved on. A handful of us went to college, the majority to the workforce, many to the military, a good number to California, and, unfortunately, some to prison. Yet, whenever our paths crossed, we called back the memory of that spontaneous and magical parade and the block party organized and staged on Durango Street by residents of the Westside.

SQUARE HEADS

I would learn about our new neighbors only when I overheard my father tell my mother that they were *cabezas cuadradas* or square heads. I recalled Papa Mundo saying, "*Si Ruby, son alemanes. ¿Qué dices Edmundo?*"

She asked, "*¿De que estas hablando?*"

My father responded, "*Te digo que los nuevos vecinos son alemanes.*"

I couldn't believe what I'd heard; I never knew there were people with square heads and could hardly wait to see them.

My friends were talking about them. María, my friend, who lived down the street, came to tell me, "Your new neighbors across the street are *animales.*"

"What are you talking about?" And she repeated. "Your neighbors across the street are *animales.*"

As the second hand on a clock, Mama Ruben who went to hang clothes said, "*No, no, María, son alemanes,*" stressing the correct pronunciation.

"Yes, that's what I said, *animales.*" Spanish for "animals" was the only sound that came out.

For the next few days — ever the curious investigator — I spent most afternoons spying on the Germans. But I never saw them.

Eventually, I gave up. I went on with my life.

Then one day, quite by chance, I spotted them. I stared to the point of turning cross-eyed. My disappointment was to find out their heads were like ours. I wondered, "What was my father thinking?"

A couple of weeks after they moved in, Mama and I walked over to meet our neighbors, with a big piping hot bowl of *arroz con pollo* chicken and rice that had just come off the stove. When Candace opened the door, my mother said, "Excuse me but I don't speak German, *el Aleman.*" Candace looked puzzled and I sort of translated.

She laughed and said, "Oh, good! Because I don't either." I think that's when Candace and Mama became life-long friends.

Ted and Candace whom we now called Connie lived in the big old house with Mr. Mac, who was Connie's brother, and Grandma. Because they weren't Mexican American, we viewed them with apprehension and reservation. We weren't used to having neighbors who weren't like us, you know, who had a different culture and who didn't speak Spanish.

Talk in the neighborhood was that they were driven off their land by the government because it needed their property. In recompense, they were offered the lot next to our house and paid to move their house into the lot. If fighting the government wasn't enough, it was whispered that family violence was involved.

Connie later shared a story about a night of serious drinking and fighting. Someone in the family had shot somebody else in self-defense. Connie retold the story with the caveat that it was "unlike my oldest brother. He was as mean as a hornet's nest and then some—but you would've never met a better person." Of course, Mama didn't know what to say and asked Connie if she wanted something to eat; Mama believed a good meal solved all problems.

The Warner family turned out to be generous, friendly, and caring neighbors who kept a tidy house and yard. Like them, my mother and grandmother were sergeants and shared a predilection for order and everything in its place. Connie was a Baptist and one day she decided to invite my mother to Bible study. Mama was shocked and said, "Candace, soy Católica. I'm Catholic."

Candace replied, "I know you're Catholic, dear. I'm not trying to convert you, or anything. It's fun. And people bring their best dishes."

Upon hearing about the food, Mama said, "I'll go." Candace turned to my grandmother and told her she should come too. Mama kept going to Bible studies until the sessions ended. She looked forward to hanging out with the Baptists for a couple of hours, every Monday.

One day Mama announced that if we wanted to go out that night, we needed to clean the house, pronouncing, "'A clean mind and body can never be clean enough,' says the Lord."

Yolanda, my oldest sister, smiled and said, "Mom, don't you mean 'Cleanliness is next to Godliness?'"

"Sí. Algo así. Something like that," she replied and walked away.

Yolanda and I looked at each other, and said, "Great. Now it's those Baptists!"

Dan Warner spent most days working in the yard while dressed in his favorite uniform: blue overalls and old Army boots. Candance spent most days baking and Dan walked to the local ice station to drink beer. Together, they pitched in and took care of their grandma until she died. They were proud to never have sent Grandma to an "old folk's home."

The Warner's became an extension of our family. They came to all our parties, birthdays, graduations, weddings, showers, baptisms, and anniversaries. After Sunday church services, my parents often went to their house for lunch, and their generosity came through in many ways. For example, Candance found out about the girls' birthdays, and like clockwork, she came over to drop off our gifts. Her brother couldn't even wait for a birthday; throughout the year, he surprised us with presents.

Some years later, Candace's brother took ill and died. My family felt his loss. We missed seeing him sitting out in his backyard and listening to his stories about World War I. Years later, after a brief illness, Candace passed away. My mother worried about Dan; she said it was heartbreaking to lose your lifelong partner and that we couldn't understand until we walked down that road. Twice during the week, and on Sundays, my mother set aside some food for Dan. With every plate he would laugh and say, "I still have leftover food from last week. I think Ruby is trying to fatten me up." When Dan passed, a daughter by his first marriage who lived in another state sold the Warner homestead—a home that held many memories for me.

Every time I visited my mother, I would look across the street at this beautiful, old home that lovingly brought memories of our German friends—the family whose house magically appeared across the street and became part of my life. We lost our almost-family, but we would soon gain other ways to find the fun in life.

WESTSIDE HOME

TV
VENDING
MACHINE

"*No quiero* endeudarme Edmundo. ¡Odio las trácalas." To make her point, I heard Mama Ruben translating her words, as if to emphasize she really meant it. "I don't want to get in debt. I hate debt."

Papa Mundo replied, "Yes, but I want us to have a TV Ruby, and if we don't get in debt, we'll never have anything, you know, it's like, you know, the American dream."

Mother responded, "We have everything we need."

"I know. But a TV would be nice for the kids," my father added.

Mama said, "No. The kids are fine, they listen to the radio, and they ride their bikes and skates all around the neighborhood. We don't need a TV."

"No. No—let me tell you how we're going to pay. Just listen. I think you'll change your mind—" At that exact moment, my friends showed up with their bikes and I ran out to join them.

A few days later, I walked in and saw my brothers relocating our furniture. I asked them why and they said, "We're making room for our new TV."

I couldn't believe it. We were going to be one of the first families to have a TV.

Since my mother refused to buy anything for which she hadn't saved up, it was a miracle. I could hear her words: "Once you start owing people, you become their slaves; you no longer work for yourself but for them. We may not have much, but we have peace of mind and that's worth more than anything we can buy on credit."

I'll never forget the day they delivered our TV. I spent the entire day running out into the street mentally willing the arrival of the delivery truck. When it showed up, I was exhausted.

Two men dressed in gray uniforms carried a large, square-shaped box into our living room. Inside the box was our brand spanking new nineteen-inch, black and white Philco. The men instructed Mama Ruben and me on how to operate it. She stood there and I simply stared at the TV, not hearing a word the men said. My only wish was for them to leave so we could turn it on.

Once the men left, I begged Mama Ruben. "Turn it on. Turn it on."

She said, "We have to wait until Papa Mundo gets home. Besides, we don't have any money."

"Why would we need money?" I didn't understand what she meant. I told her we didn't need money to watch TV. She insisted we did.

As she walked out, Mama Ruben turned around and told me, "Don't touch it. It's not a toy."

Then I heard her pulling out pots and pans in the kitchen to start cooking. I kicked off my black and white Oxfords and silently tippy toed to the TV turned every knob on and pushed every button. Nothing worked. I gave up and went outside to play, convinced we had wasted good hard-earned money for a good-for-nothing television. We'd been duped!

As soon as my friends saw me, they ran over to grill me about the delivery truck. I responded, "We bought a TV." Of course, they

FRIENDS AND FAMILY GETTING READY
FOR THE WRESTLING SHOW

wanted to see it. But I added, "Until my father comes home from work, we can't turn it on. He wants us to watch it as family for the first time." I didn't want them to know our parents had purchased a brand-new broken-down TV.

When Papa Mundo came home, he immediately went over to the TV to inspect it. He took out some quarters and went behind the TV and slipped them somewhere. Magically, it came on. I couldn't believe my eyes. I worked! It worked with quarters! Oh my gosh, we had to feed this TV one quarter per hour of watching. What a joke. Then I thought, "Since I've never been this close to a TV, maybe they are all like ours." That must've been it.

Every Friday afternoon, the TV man showed up to extract the quarters or his weekly payment. My mother loved this plan.

After church on Sundays, Gilbert and Stella Carreño, the *compadres* showed at our house for lunch. Very *simpatico*, and always wearing a suit, *el compadre* removed his hat to step inside. He enjoyed watching TV while the *comadre* helped Mama Ruben in the kitchen. The TV, like clockwork, would turn off every hour on the hour. Without hesitation, *compa* stood up, fed the TV, and got it going again. He was a major donor of our weekly payment.

Wednesday was wrestling night. Friends and neighbors came to watch the TV that now faced towards an open window, and the neighbors arranged their kitchen chairs to get the best view. Sometimes there were fifteen or twenty whooping, hollering, and placing bets for their favorite wrestler. Hourly, our TV demanded payment and people would jump out of their seat to feed it.

Whether or not families brought snacks and drinks to share, they were welcomed. Mother was in awe that no matter how many people showed up or how little food there was, everyone was served just like in the Bible story. The women spent those evenings catching-up with the weekly happenings. Of course, their visits included the latest neighborhood gossip. The kids were left to run wild and ran after lightning bugs or chased one another down Durango and Rosillo Streets. Tired, we would sit on someone's yard to rest and comb the sky for shooting stars until it was time to go home.

After we got our TV, we fell into a routine. First, our chores and homework. Then we gathered around that nineteen-inch set to watch our favorite shows: Mama and Mama Tere loved the Lawrence Welk and Groucho Marx Shows, Papa Mundo loved wrestling, my brothers preferred the Lone Ranger, and my sisters dug American Bandstand. I, too, would rush home to watch my favorite program, the Mickey Mouse Club. My ritual was to sneak into Mama Ruben's bureau and grab her black padded strapless bra to simulate Mickey Mouse ears. I happily sat on the floor, crossed my legs, and snapped the bra straps under my chin to sing along.

As more families purchased their own TVs—which didn't take quarters to work—our Wednesday night neighborhood wrestling parties faded. After a while, everyone was inside their own homes watching their programs. Months later, several neighbors came by and told my parents they missed the weekly gatherings and wanted to restart them. For the next couple of years, we continued to enjoy this neighborhood tradition that brought people out of their homes and into our backyard.

In the end, my mother told Papa Mundo, "Amor, you were so intelligente to buy that TV; it was so easy to pay off! Now, what else are you going to buy for us?" Then she showered his face with soft, gentle kisses.

SCHOOL
BEGINS

As reliable as the noon ringing bells of Sacred Heart that announced the Angelus, my grandmother Mama Tere woke at 5:30 to recite her morning prayers. Her whispering prayers often woke me. However, I readily dozed back off until she finally got me out of bed with the soft pounding of the *palote* that she used to stretch out a stack of flour tortillas for breakfast and our lunch bags.

Today was a special day. I was starting school.

For a very long time I had been waiting for this day. As the youngest of six, I was tired of watching my siblings run off to school each morning as they left me behind. I was ready to learn how to read and write. In my child mind, I wondered if I was smart enough, or if I would make new friends. I was for sure certain I would be the best student!

When the time came for me to go to school, I boldly announced that no one had to walk me. After all, my elementary school was but a block away and I often walked there to play with my friends. I *would be just fine!* Ready, I picked up my new Big Chief tablet and Number 2 pencils and headed out. I waved at Mama Ruben and Mama Tere who kept an eye on me from our front porch as I walked to school. This new adventure filled me with excitement, love, and joy.

TERESA, EARLY SCHOOL YEARS

Although I remember much about those early years, I'll never forget that all my teachers were Anglo females. Still, the majority were kind and they taught me the ABCs, reading, writing, numbers, and dance.

Whenever we took a test, I'd get so nervous that I could barely breathe much less control the shaking of my hand and pencil as I wrote. At times, I held the pencil with both hands to steady it, and I wanted to throw up.

My favorite games to play during recess were hopscotch, jacks, and what we called *el chicote*—those times we locked arms with each other and swung in one direction, picking up speed until the chain broke. While my recollections are brief, I will forever remember my new friend Carmela. She had beautiful caramel-colored skin and eyes, smiled sweetly, spoke no English, and sat next to me. One day, not too long after we were given instructions, my friend asked, "*¿Qué dice?*" When the teacher walked away, I softly translated for my friend.

But when the teacher heard our whispers in Spanish, she returned to tell us, "If you continue speaking Spanish, you will be punished."

As she turned around, I placed my index finger against my lips. Motioning for my friend to hush, I reinforced the "no speaking Spanish" rule.

Contrarily, the teacher instructed me. "Now, tell her exactly what I said."

How could I? We were prohibited from speaking Spanish. Given the tears that tumbled down my friend's cheeks, I was sure she felt the rejection.

When the teacher turned to face the classroom all the students stared at her bug-eyed. Some nodded yes, while others gestured no.

The teacher, not knowing if we meant, "Yes, we will speak Spanish" or "No we will not speak Spanish," turned bright red and abruptly headed back to her desk. She didn't understand that we wanted to please her.

We only wanted to follow the marching orders we were given at home: "Respect your *maestra*. Do what she says, *o ya veras* or you'll feel the consequences."

After this I put my head down and became quiet and withdrawn. I wanted to avoid trouble. I learned to follow orders as this would make me the best student. After that, I never spoke much. Sure, I responded when the teacher called on me, but never volunteered. When students were threatened and paddled for speaking Spanish, I said nothing.

We were just kids. When school was over and the bell rang, all was forgotten and forgiven, so I thought. We would jump out of our seats and ran out of the building laughing, skipping, pushing, and teasing until we reached the safety of our home.

My friends and I never told our parents what was going on at school. We were taught to respect our elders, especially since most of us had one and sometimes even two beloved *abuelas* living with us. We believed that the teachers were only doing what they thought was best for us. After all, they were the adults. We were mere children.

Along with other students, Carmela, with her ready smile, made every effort to learn English. But inside the classroom, she spent most her school days in a fog unless one of us helped her. Before Christmas break, Carmela vanished and never returned to school. For the rest of the year, every time I glanced at her empty chair I felt sadness and shame.

More difficulties would emerge in those schools that targeted and separated us. Humiliation would become par for the course in our educational journey.

PIOJOS
AND
TEACHERS

A few months after school began, I heard my teacher yell, "Head check. Head check. Get ready for the head check."

I thought, "What the heck is a head check?"

We were told to line up along the classroom wall in alphabetical order, and, at the back of the line, I stood on my tippy toes, craning my neck to see what was going on. Some of my friends were laughing. Some were fidgeting. Others were close to tears. Each one of us was trying to figure out what was going on. As the line got shorter, I saw my teacher wearing plastic gloves with sticks in her hands. With a look of disgust, she was rummaging through our hair: straight hair, curly hair, short and wavy hair, unruly hair, clean hair, and dirty hair. Besides being a teacher, she was *chota* in the *piojo* police.

The boy in front of me excitedly said, "They are looking for *piojos* or lice." My heart pounded inside my chest, and I felt my temperature rise.

My friend Martha who was standing next to me laughingly teased, "Why are you so red? You look like a candied apple." It was easy to ignore her comment, but my mind imagined hundreds of tiny feet marching on my scalp. I hid my hands tightly as I wished nothing more than to scratch the imaginary itch. Not wanting to draw attention to myself, I refrained even though I imagined zillions of *piojos* all over my scalp. We were all suspect. I tried to figure out who had lice and who didn't. Then I recalled using another girl's hairbrush. I wanted to puke. This time Martha said I was turning the color of a pickle. I was so scared I felt like crying.

To this day, I don't know what kept me in that stupid line; what kept me from darting out of the room and running home. After all, I lived a block away. One short block away. I reasoned I could've had Mama Ruben check my head before I got to the front of the line and that way, I would confirm that I didn't have lice and forgo the humiliation. Bet I could've gone and returned before the teacher even missed me.

As the line inched forward, my heart was doing a marathon. Some kids now had notes in their hands and were told to go home. I figured those were the one hundred percent *piojentos*. I was 99.99 percent sure I didn't have *piojos*. But what if I did? If the teacher handed me a note and sent me home, I would've dropped out of school or at the very least left for a school where no one knew me. Before long my chest felt as tight as if a bull was sitting on it, and my breathing became labored. I was very, very close to passing out.

Despite all my riled-up emotions, I got to the front of the line. The teacher told me to sit in a large wooden chair that faced the front of the class. She checked my hair. When she was done, she told me to go sit down. I gladly translated this into "No *piojos*!" Soon, my breathing slowed, and I could feel myself relaxing. Shortly, I returned to the business of school. Maybe I wouldn't drop out after all.

The following Monday several parents showed up at school with their children and demanded to see the principal. We would find out that the parents told the principal the teacher had mistaken dandruff for lice and unnecessarily embarrassed their children. From then on, I kept my distance from my peers, you know, just in case.

"BOLO," PADRINO, "BOLO"

On that soft, sagging mattress with Mama Lita, my maternal grandmother, and my brother Jesse at the foot of the bed with his nose against my stinky feet, my head pressed against the massive, ancient headboard. I felt Jesse squirm and softly count the tolling of the church bells one-by-one. At the count of seven, my brother jumped out and screamed, "Get up Teresita. It's seven. We have to go to church." Hastily, I went to change my pajamas for my clothes and slipped my feet in my worn and tight-fitting shoes.

Mama Lita lived in the heart of San Antonio's Westside, directly across from Our Lady of Guadalupe Church (OLG). After our mother passed, Jesse, who was two years older than me and almost three years of age at the time, went to live with our maternal grandmother and our uncle Tío Chuy. Today was a special church day. It was Baptismal Sunday, and Jesse, a young eight-year-old and me, a mature six-year-old, loved going to church. My brother and I ran across the street to wait for the baptismal families to arrive.

All the children were dressed in their Sunday best and made every effort not to get dirty for fear of getting in trouble. But the most beautifully dressed were the babies. They wore long white

SANTUARIO OF THE VIRGEN DE GUADALUPE

gowns made of linen with lace and some even had matching coats and bonnets; they truly looked angelic. This was the day children were turned over to our Lord, thus they had to look like they were made in heaven.

The parents, *padrinos, abuelas y abuelos, tías* and *tíos*, and a slew of kids of all ages came dressed in their Sunday best. The men wore their perfectly pressed but dated suits, spit-shined Stacy Adams, and stylish fedora hats. The women dressed in colorful crepe dresses and wore high-heeled shoes. When they got to the church, they reached into their handbags to pull out their silk *mantillas* and covered their heads right before entering. Women parishioners knew not to walk into Father Tranchese's church without their veil. He was known for honoring the rules as zealously as he protected the neighborhood's families, cultures, and traditions.

Along with the neighborhood children, Jesse and I waited for the families to exit. We knew a treat was coming our way: coins, or what we knew as *bolo*, would rain from heaven. When the families came out we rushed towards them yelling, "Bolo, *padrinos*, bolo." My brother grabbed my hand and said "Don't let go." I held on tightly as he muscled us into the front.

We loved this ritual. In celebration of this joyous occasion, and to show intent to provide religious and financial support to their godchild if and when the parents couldn't, the *padrinos* reached deep into their pockets and threw fists full of coins high up in the air. For an instant, the coins appeared to be suspended mid-flight and we could almost guess the worth of each coin. When the sun's rays showered the coins with light, it looked like it was gold.

We scrambled to pick up what we could before they were all scooped up. In our handmade cloth sacks, we filled what we could.

JESSE AND TERESA GETTING READY FOR BOLO TIMES

Once Jesse and I amassed our fortune, we huddled together to count our booty. I wished for enough to pay for a movie and even a little extra for two cookies, or a candy, which we would cut into two pieces and share.

These Sunday morning celebrations set us up for our special afternoons. Fifty cents of *bolo* bought us fun at the Guadalupe, or *El Progreso*, but our neighborhood theater visits would cease when the unexpected happened. One morning as Jesse darted across the street to collect his *bolo*, he was hit by a car. Tío Chuy's forewarning came true! "*Mucho cuidado, te va a machucar un carro*, be very careful a car is going to run you over." Fortunately, my brother wasn't hurt, but that was the end of *bolo* days. After the accident we became spectators.

EL PROGRESO, NEIGHBORHOOD THEATER,
AND MAMA TERE'S CONCESSION STAND,
COURTESY OF THE UTSA DIGITAL COLLECTION

FEAST DAY OF OUR LADY OF GUADALUPE

The day before the feast day of Our Lady of Guadalupe was a busy one in our home as we rushed around to get ready for the procession.

"Mama," I called out, "*¿Dónde está mi vestido blanco y mi corona?*"

"*Busca en el* cedar chest, *en mi cuarto,*" she answered.

Once I found it, Mama Ruben washed and ironed my white—now slightly yellowed dress—and replaced the little yellow flowers on my crown with small red roses and long flowing ribbons in honor of our *Guadalupana*. Mama then prepared a small bouquet of red roses to present to the *Virgencita* on her feast day.

My sister Janie was also busy rummaging through her clothes to find something white to wear for the celebration. After she picked out a dress, we packed our clothes into a small cloth satchel and walked to Mama Lita's house, which was directly across the OLG Church in San Antonio's Westside, to spend the night. We wanted to be close by to witness the entire festivity.

Sometime before midnight, I awoke to the measured sounds of trumpets and the soft strumming of guitars, violins, harps, violoncellos, accordions, and other instruments. When midnight came, the church bells tolled. A symphony of music and singing erupted as dozens of musicians gathered on the plaza to begin their *serenata* serenade of *Las Mañanitas* to our Lady of Guadalupe. We sat on our porch across the street with our *familia* wearing pajamas and winter coats and we joined the singing. Throughout those early morning hours, dressed in their beautiful *trajes* and *charro* hats, one *mariachi* group after another went about singing to our Lady. We continued to watch and participate, and then Tío Chuy brought small clay cups filled with *Champurrado* to keep us warm. The neighbors came out to watch and listen.

Around 4 o'clock in the morning, people gathered several blocks away to take their place in the procession leading to the church, the home of our beloved. My sister and I wore our white dresses in honor of our mother and her two sisters, who in their *juventud* youth had been *Hijas de María* at this same church.

When Janie asked Mama Lita if she was going to join us she replied, "No *hijas, no tengo animo; yo las espero en la iglesia*. No child, I don't have the wherewithal; I'll wait for you at the church." Jesse, in his proud *monaguillo* altar boy attire, stood next to Mama Lita. I started to plead with her, but Janie put her index finger on her lips, to shush me. As we walked to take our place at the end of the line, my sister told me that it was too painful for our grandmother to walk without our beautiful Mother and two aunts alongside her, as they had done for many years.

That December 12th was an exceptionally cold morning, but it didn't keep people from showing up to be part of this sacred day. A sea of people came. People from down the street and throughout the city. Catholics, and non-Catholics, young and old, people in wheelchairs or crutches, and mothers held their babies tightly swaddled in their *reboso* shawls against their breast to keep them warm. Younger children were strolled, and toddlers were taken in hand-pulled wagons with colorful wool blankets wrapped around them.

Some men dressed in white with traditional *zarapes* draped over their shoulders, just like Juan Diego wore that fateful day when our Blessed Mother appeared to him on that hill of Tepeyac near Mexico City as he tended to his duties. Little boys made their way to the church dressed like their fathers with small mustaches painted with their mother's eyebrow pencil or shoeshine. To express their love and devotion for our Virgin of Guadalupe, a crowd of people left their warm *casitas* and descended upon that poor, humble church located in one of oldest neighborhoods of San Antonio.

As the procession inched forward, like gently rolling waves, people began singing. They held up their personal statues of our Lady—some made of clay, some carved out of wood—and others carried framed pictures of the *Guadalupana* that had been in their family for many generations. Some wore thin or thick silver or gold chains around their necks with their OLG medals, with the expectation to get them blessed. Red, white, and green streamers of ribbon—the colors of the land where she appeared—were tied to long poles and gently flew above us. Organizations proudly carried their mostly white and gold banners: *Hijas de María*, OLG Altar Society, and Knights of Columbus were all up-front and ready to be first to enter the church for the commemorative mass.

A couple of blocks before we arrived, the procession came to a stop. The church and the plaza overflowed with people who had begun praying to our Blessed Mother. Sometime later, the *peregrinos* or pilgrims marched forward, and everyone entered the church to spend a few minutes with our Lady. Three men who had started walking on their knees from the street curb arrived at the altar with bloodied knees. Mama Lita said these men were paying *una manda muy grande* or making good on a big promise they'd made. When it was our turn to kneel before OLG to present our bouquet of roses, I saw a pile of letters, lists of names and petitions, rosaries, *milagros* in the shape of hearts, and pictures at her feet. Those roses would adorn the altar for months to come.

We came to thank the *Virgencita* for her intercessions and to acknowledge her for the times she said "Yes," and even the times she said "No." We showed our appreciation for the strength to face hard times, poor health, difficult relationships, lost children, estranged family, joblessness, and uncertainty. We professed our love and gave thanks for the spiritual sustenance she provided. And, as people got up to leave, tears of joy ran down their faces. This unbridled expression of love, of raw emotion, of total surrender, stirred even those whose hearts were stone cold.

Once people took their leave, they mingled at the plaza with a cup of coffee, hot chocolate, and pastries, and lacked the desire to leave. People of faith gathered to honor Our Lady of Guadalupe on her feast day—one of several yearly Westside celebrations that made our side of town a unique and special community. Even when we experienced pervasive poverty and crime like other areas across town, we had the comfort of this small plot of holy land at 1321 El Paso, Our Lady of Guadalupe Church, where our *Virgencita Morena, la madre de México*, our Lady, *Reina de las Americas*—our *Guadalupana* was there to remind us to be kind, generous, accepting, tolerant, and above all loving. She was our comfort and our salvation.

In our view, Our Lady of Guadalupe was accepting and forgiving, even to those who had to make difficult personal choices. Like our family doctor, our Lupita was there to heal our spirit and give us peace.

DOCTOR TREAT'S HOUSE CALLS

Mama Tere had been sick for a few days. Soon, Mama Ruben contacted our family doctor, calling the number of his small clinic located behind Walter's Pharmacy on Commerce Street. Good thing Dr. Treat made house calls and would be stopping by our house. This made me go I into panic mode and I frantically looked around to secure a hiding place, as I thought "What if the doctor suddenly realized I was due for a shot and wanted to take care of it right here and now, while he examined Mama Tere?

Then, I heard, "*¿Ya llego el doctor?* The doctor has arrived?" Those warning words made me dive into the pitch-dark hall closet where I left a small crack to let in the light.

In the protection of the closet's darkness, I heard the doctor tell Mama Ruben, "I'm giving her a shot that will make her feel much better."

I thought, "Why does he always have to give shots?" I couldn't remember one time that I had gone in to see him that he didn't give me a shot. Just once, once, I wanted him to say, "You don't need a shot today." But no, each time we saw him, out came the cotton balls, alcohol, and that dreaded needle I deeply despised.

Right after graduating from medical school, Dr. Treat opened his practice in the Westside, spending many years serving families in our Prospect Hill neighborhood. Always jovial, he quickly learned a rudimentary Spanish to communicate with his patients. To save us money, Dr. Treat often gave Mama Tere medicine samples, and he would give me coupons for a free ice-cream cone at Walter's Pharmacy.

There were times when Mama Ruben wondered out loud, "¿*Cómo el doctor* could make a living in a neighborhood where most people wanted to pay him with homemade *tamales*, fresh eggs from their chicken coops, or promissory notes to pay *mañana* tomorrow?" Still, for years, Dr. Treat tended young and old, the poor and the destitute. When patients were too sick to go to his clinic, he went to their homes. Mama always said that his generous spirit was as large as his stature because he was a tall and chunky man.

Sadly, the word spread that Dr. Treat performed abortions when and if a woman desperately requested it, even when these procedures were illegal. He also treated his share of women who tried to self-abort or saw those that had been mutilated by untrained persons at squalid places. Before long word reached the police, and Dr. Treat was arrested, sent to prison, and lost his medical license.

Many years later, Dr. Treat showed up at our front door with a petition to get his license back. My mother immediately signed on and told him to leave her a sheet or two to gather additional signatures.

He was quite surprised and thanked her over and over by stating, "You are a good woman, Ruby. I admire you for taking in all your nieces and nephews and caring for your elderly mother all these years. I loved working in this community, people are just so real and kind." Mama blushed and told him everyone was sad when he left, and that people missed him. He gave Mama his card with a new address, so she could mail him the petition. True to her word, Mama combed the neighborhood for days until she filled two pages with signatures. To mail them, she went to the Post office downtown with Papa.

Mama didn't believe in abortion, but she didn't want Dr. Treat to continue suffering for having helped women who found themselves in desperate situations. Years later, after he left us the petition, Papa Mundo read an article in the Express-News, announcing that Dr. Treat had died in a car accident in Houston. People in our neighborhood who had been recipients of his generosity were upset the article only focused on his arrest record, rather than on the many years of service he gave to the Westside community. Our neighborhoods, like many others, experienced difficult times when those we cared for opted for choices that led to their death.

NEIGHBOR'S SUICIDE

It was just another ordinary Saturday morning. I never thought it would end that way. Sad to say, we lost a lonely old man who was our neighbor.

I'd been riding my bicycle around my neighborhood for a good hour or two and was on my way home when I noticed a small group of people huddled together in the back alley across the street from my house. As I got closer, my friend María rode her bike to meet me and told me that our neighbor Mr. Martin had just shot himself in the head.

"Hurry up and come see his body before the ambulance takes him away. He's all full of blood and he hasn't moved. I think he's dead, and you can see some of his brains."

As she rattled off all the unwanted and gory details, my mind tried to make sense of what she was saying. I tried to decipher what she said and thought, "Who is she talking about? None of my neighbors would do such a thing."

Then, Mama Tere's *dicho* echoed inside my mind. "*¡Que no se te cierre el mundo!* Don't let the world close in on you."

My words finally came out as I warned María, "Slow down. Stop.

What are you talking about?"

She answered, "I told you, *Señor* Martin." My mind was still in a state of confusion, desperately trying to grasp her yapping.

I'd been at his house a few weeks ago playing with his two grandchildren. They both played piano, guitar, and had strong singing voices. After they entertained their grandfather with their music, we went to the backyard which had several half-built structures we enjoyed exploring. When we were in one of the dilapidated sheds, I picked up a dirty bottle and pretended there was a genie inside. I brought it to my left eye then a swarm of bees flew out and attacked my face. I screamed and ran home. There, to relieve the pain and swelling, Mama Tere put together one of her healing ointments.

I couldn't believe this was happening and my mind was all over the place. I asked myself, "Hadn't I just seen him working in his flower garden when I rode my bike past his house earlier today? Or was that yesterday?" I didn't know if it was today or yesterday or the day before — not that it mattered now.

Then, I suddenly realized I would never see him again. He would never bring us flowers from his yard, and I would never hear him say, "*Buenos días*, Teresita, *¿Están todos bien?*" He'd asked me if we were doing well, something that regularly occurred whenever I walked in front of his home.

Mr. Martin's wife, Margarita, had been sick for many years and had passed away a year before. He had been living all alone but had told my parents that his son and family were going to move in with him so he would have someone there. Could it have been they decided not to move? Surely, that wouldn't have driven him to take his own life. I wondered, "What had?"

María grabbed my arm and started to pull me over to where Mr. Martin was laying on the ground. I kept resisting. I had no desire to see him that way. Eventually, she gave up. But as I slowly walked my bike next to the alley, I glanced over to where his body rested and I froze. There was blood on the right side of his head. His arms and legs were skewed, rigid, and looked oddly uncomfortable. I noticed he was wearing his brown suit, black tie, and a pair of spit-shined, going-out shoes, as if he wanted to meet his maker in his best clothes.

One of our compassionate neighbors covered him with a blue Mexican woolen blanket. "Thank God for that!" Mr. Martin was a very proud man. He wouldn't have wanted a bunch of people staring at him. Some of the women prayed and several men paced up and down the street and waited for his body to be picked up by the coroner. When I looked over to our house, my mother and grandmother were standing in the front porch. I was glad they hadn't walked over. That night Mama Tere gathered our family and a few close neighbors, and we prayed a rosary for his soul.

Several months after Mr. Martin's suicide, María swore that whenever she was in the alley she would see Mr. Martin walking around asking for help and saying, "It'd all been a big mistake."

According to her, "He walks around with his arms stretched out, just like a zombie."

I said, using the nickname our neighborhood kids had given her and which she detested, "Stop it, Mamoleque." I seldom resorted to the use of this name as I was her friend, but today was the right day to use it because she was being hateful. I reminded her Mama Tere always said that we better respect the dead: "O, *ya verán* or you'll pay." Still, Mamoleque continued torturing the little kids in the neighborhood with the ghost story, including me, until I ignored her. Then she stopped.

I never knew whether to believe her loose talk about him walking around like a zombie or not. I only knew that the memory of him lying dead in the alley, full of blood and dirt, dressed up like a *catrín* gave me nightmares. This did not end until Mama Tere cured me of *susto* and gave me a spiritual cleansing to rid me of the fear.

A couple of months after Mr. Martin's suicide, María's mother asked Mama Tere to perform a *susto* healing over her daughter. She said that since Mr. Martin's death, her daughter thrashed and cried in her sleep, keeping everyone awake. Mama Tere agreed to perform the ritual. Afterwards, María and her family was able to sleep. I wasn't convinced she had deserved treatment, at least not yet. But those were confusing times for me. While I recognized her playfulness and trickster selves, I did not have the maturity of a *curandera* to understand her ways. I hope to learn some day.

While her treatment worked, Mama Tere couldn't help those who most needed her assistance. They understood a mother's love, but she was not one to enable those who followed addiction paths.

LA ADICCIÓN

No one ever figured out what happened to Pedro, although rumors spread around the neighborhood like dust devils, spinning, spinning, and spinning the so-called news. Some claimed he fell in with the wrong crowds, which was not hard to do. Many believed he was too good looking for his own good. What with his thick curly hair, chiseled face, and dimples like bottomless wells, the women often uttered, "*Pues*, forget it," adding, "Who could resist that?" His deep, melodic, intoxicating voice, drove them crazy.

"*Mira*, look," my mother's cousin commented, "He's, our Earl Flynn."

"*Nombre, está identico.*"

Another woman chimed, "He's a twin to Gary Cooper."

"No, no, no, *quítate de aquí* go away."

They all agreed, "If Clark Gable *se rasuraba ese bigotito* shaved that moustache, bingo, it's Pedro"

Life in our neighborhood was gloriously beautiful, yet treacherous. Like those thorny bougainvillea that adorned our home, some grew wild and got lost. As everywhere, drugs were readily available and lured many into a web of addiction and pain. Sadly, at a young age, Pedro fell for heroin's false promise of ecstasy and became ensnarled with its relentless cravings.

Life was just "Too easy street for Pedro," our next-door neighbor claimed, "He could get on the bus, go downtown, and get any job he wanted. Who wouldn't want him working in their store?"

"He could have any girl, or woman, even some married ones," the women would say and laugh. And then they would dreamily think about Pedro, as they glanced and pointed over to their husbands, instead of "that."

Pedro was easily the most handsome of Consuelo's sons. All agreed he would go far, what with his good looks and that baritone voice. Consuelo was our neighbor and my mother's good friend—a widow with three sons and a daughter, and her children were friends of my siblings. She was always running over to our house to have a cup of coffee with *pan dulce* and to talk about Pedro.

After she left Mama Ruben would lament, "*Pobre Consuelo, ese cuento es de nunca acabar,* for her it's the never-ending story."

When Pedro was locked up, Consuelo would ask my mother and grandmother to pray that he would survive prison and get released. My mother prayed as Consuelo asked, but my grandmother's prayer was altogether different. She prayed and then demanded that the demons release their hold over Pedro.

Every day as I walked in front of Consuelo's house to and from the bus stop on my way to school, she was either inside playing the piano or outside tending to her flowers. It was often said Consuelo had a "musical ear." She only had to hear a song once and would capture it on the piano's keys the first time. Just don't give her a sheet of music to play because she couldn't read it.

If Consuelo was gardening, she would greet me and announce, "Only 121 days to go before Pedro returns home," and the countdown would shrink daily. When it hit day zero, Pedro came home. Consuelo was so happy she threw a huge block party for him with food, drink, and *mariachis*. Everyone had a good time, although Pedro looked sad and scared. Perhaps he had learned that prison had less to do with rehabilitation and more to do with becoming hard and mean.

In time, Consuelo confided to my mother that she was worried about Pedro. He couldn't find a job and would disappear for days at a time. When she would question her son, he would explode and begin cursing and, of course, he always demanded money from Consuelo. Her children warned her not to give him any because he would use it to buy drugs, but Consuelo could not listen.

Pedro began to age and faded away right before our eyes. Every day he got skinnier, then he became gaunt. His cheek bones protruded on his face, his eyes sunk into his skull, and he began losing his hair which gave him a ghoulish look equal to those skulls that begin to appear for day of the dead. We all suspected that he had found his way back to drug hell.

When Consuelo stopped giving him money, things started to vanish from the home. Anything that could be carried off and sold was lost: jewelry, the lawnmower, a radio, the television, and their tools. One day his siblings threw Pedro out of the house and yelled, "Never come back."

Consuelo continued to suffer and soon she told my mother that she was scared Pedro was going to die in the streets. She struggled and prayed for the police to catch him and send him back to prison. In her view, that was the only way she would learn of Pedro's whereabouts.

One day as I walked past her home from the bus stop, Consuelo was wailing and screaming. I ran home and shared that something terrible might've happened to Consuelo. My mother ran over and found her friend sobbing uncontrollably.

"Pedro's body has been found under a downtown bridge."

When Mama Tere found out what had happened she exclaimed, "*Gracias a Dios, ya lo soltaron los demonios.* Thank God, the demons released him. *¡Como sufrió ese muchacho!* How that young man suffered."

As was Mama Tere's custom, a couple of days after Pedro's funeral she gathered my family, Consuelo and her children, friends, and neighbors to pray the rosary. Afterwards, we assembled for coffee and *pan dulce* while people shared their memories about Pedro. Consuelo had never heard some of the stories that were told. As I glanced at my mother's friend, I could see that the stories brought her much needed comfort.

PREMIER MOVIE HOUSE IN SAN ANTONIO

One evening, before Papa Mundo left to report to his graveyard shift at Kelly Air Force Base, he told us that he was taking us to the movies the next day and wanted us ready by noon. By 10 o'clock in the morning, my sisters and I were ready and anxiously waiting. We kept wondering if we were going to the Guadalupe Theater or perhaps the *Nacional* downtown or even the Alameda, which was by far the nicest of the three.

For the outing, Mama Ruben packed a few snacks and reminded us not to ask for soda or candy. We promised we wouldn't.

Our parents never discussed money in front of us—or rather the lack of it—even though Papa Mundo always worked two jobs. When we heard her say, "¡Lo *siento! No hay dinero.* Sorry. There's no money," when anyone of us asked for money for field trips or other incidentals. However, Mama Ruben would always find the money when my father got paid.

As soon as Papa Mundo got home and rested a while, we got in the car for the short drive downtown. We found parking and then walked two blocks to the theatre. But instead of walking to the front entrance, we went to the back alley and walked up to a small ticket counter. Papa Mundo's friend who worked with him at Kelly Air Force Base was employed part-time at the theatre and oversaw ticket sales. Dad talked to him and after a few minutes, his friend motioned us forward. We marched up many stairs until we reached the landing. We opened a door and entered. The movie had already started, and we hurriedly found four seats and quietly occupied them, so as not to disturb anyone.

Soon my oldest sister Yolanda said there would be an intermission and whispered that we should eat our snacks before the lights came on. We took out our fruit and cookies and ate quickly and quietly. We were afraid the lights would come on and expose us before we were finished eating.

When the lights came on and our eyes adjusted, my sisters and I were shocked to see that we were the only Mexican Americans there—the rest were what we called Negros or Blacks at the time. I could tell they were just as shocked to see us sitting there. Then, we got into an eye war. They ogled us, and we stared at them.

However, as my eyes scanned the people sitting in that balcony, I began to notice the variety of skin colors. Some people were the color of dark chocolate, some caramel, and some were nearly white. And several had light eyes. "Just like in my family," I thought. My oldest sister had the darkest skin color (yet I thought she was the prettiest), my oldest brother was white (that's why everyone called him *Güero*), and the rest of us were somewhere in the middle.

To break up our stare off, Papa Mundo told us to go up to the railing to look at the theatre. It was stunning. My eyes couldn't take in all the beauty—the intricate wood carvings, all the lighting, the imposing ceiling with bright stars and moving clouds, and the thick red

THE MAJESTIC THEATER,
COURTESY OF THE UTSA DIGITAL COLLECTION

velvet curtains covering the screen. We were sitting so high that
I felt as though I could reach up and grab a star out of the theater's sky.

The movie started again, and we went back to our seats. At the
end, we all marched back down the stairs, into the alley, down the
street, and into our car. But instead of going straight home, Papa
Mundo took us to Coney Island, an iconic downtown tiny hot dog
place that sold a hotdog and a drink for twenty-five cents. After we
ate, we looked at one another and laughed. He looked at us and said,
"Don't tell Ruby."

This was the first of many times we went to this gorgeous
theatre. We became friends with the children of my father's co-
worker and together we would go upfront to marvel at the beautiful
space. We also shared snacks.

Years later, I asked Papa Mundo about the theatre in the alley
which we frequented. He explained that Blacks were only allowed
to watch movies in the uppermost balcony and that they could only
enter the theatre through the alley. He said that his good friend at
Kelly let us in free of charge and that was the only way he could take
us to the Majestic Theater—the fanciest movie house in town.

WESTSIDE
NEIGHBORHOOD
DOGS

Movies were not our only entertainment; our fun also came from the dogs of our neighborhood. Life for the dogs wasn't all that plush because they survived on leftovers and lived under our houses. But some became our pets.

No one remembers how Scotty came to us. He just showed up. One crisp Autumn morning my grandmother, Mama Tere, opened the back door to our house and asked, "*¿De quién es este perro feo?* Whose ugly dog is this?" There, on our doorstep, was a small, curly-haired mutt rolled up tightly as a gigantic furry caterpillar like a cotton ball.

"He came from where all Westside dogs come from," I yelled. "From the back of old, rusty, noisy, back-firing pick-up trucks or cars."

Since our house was on a corner and my bed was pushed up against a window facing the side street, I witnessed many trucks or cars slowly drive by in the cover of night to push, pull, nudge, carry, or downright throw out a dog or two. Then, they would speed off. Some people didn't even wait for nighttime. They would come by any time of day to get rid of their dogs: old dogs, mangy dogs, three-legged dogs, young yapping dogs, blind dogs, and puppies, to the point that we would bet our favorite marble that the stuffed burlap sack would be full of recently born pups.

"No *tienen vergüenza* they have no shame," Mama Ruben said when she saw another abandoned dog.

Mama Tere would tell her, "No *juzgues*, don't judge," and remind us that some people couldn't feed themselves much less their dogs. Then she'd say, "*Dales el caldo de ayer* or give them yesterday's soup."

Younger dogs often ran after the vehicle until their legs gave out. When they couldn't run no more they'd plop themselves onto the street. The older dogs, on the other hand, would only stare at their owners as they drove off then lie down by the curb, rest, and grieve until they found a new home and got on with their lives.

Most of these throw-away dogs soon found new places to live in our neighborhood—underneath a house, on a porch, next to a shed, beneath a car, or under the cool shade of trees. If you gave any dog the least bit of food or water, or made eye-to-eye contact, then that dog would be yours for life. If you hoped to get rid of them, the best policy was to pretend they were not there.

For fear of being left behind again, some dogs refused to belong to anyone. Those abandoned ones roamed the neighborhood, played and fought with other dogs, and prowled for things to eat and drink. They were mostly harmless—except when a girl dog was in heat, it was then that all hell broke loose.

Neighbors only called the pound if a dog bit someone. We all knew what awaited them at the dog pound—gas. And word around the Westside was that dogs were killed and fed to lions at the zoo. When the dog catchers showed up, dogs would instinctively run and hide their faces until the truck left. Occasionally, though, the dog catchers would get lucky and haul off a few dogs and cats at a time to the dreaded place.

No one in our neighborhood ever bought a dog. Why would anyone spend their hard-earned money on a dog? A dog would most likely become yours when it showed up at your doorstep. Westside dogs lived outside—never, never inside—unless you snuck them in when no one was looking. There was a definite pecking order in our neighborhood and the order was people inside, dogs outside. For that reason, dogs didn't chew our furniture, steal our shoes, or gnaw our clothes.

Dogs did eat very well in our neighborhood with our home-cooked leftovers, and even those who didn't have their own dogs threw their leftovers over the fence for the neighborhood dogs. That good food kept many dogs alive in the Westside.

However, our dog Scotty was a picky eater. He didn't like left over *caldo*; he detested that soup. He also didn't like beans. How could a dog that didn't love beans end up in the heart of San Antonio's Westside? On the days that we would feed him *caldo* or beans, Scotty refused to eat and waited to see what our next-door neighbor thew over the fence.

Scotty became Mama Tere's dog from the first sight of him, and Scotty followed her wherever she went. If she went to visit a neighbor or walked to church or to the grocery store, there went Scotty. For being a good dog, every afternoon, my grandmother would buy Scotty a vanilla ice cream cup from the ice cream truck that passed by our house playing that horribly annoying music. That sound would get him howling up and down the yard to let us know the truck was coming miles before we heard or saw the truck.

I taught Scotty how to sit, lay down, and shake hands. I also tried a few simple lessons in Spanish "*Siéntate* or sit," I would say, but he just looked at me. Then I tried, "*Dame la mano* or give me your paw," and he would just stare. I guess he didn't know that *mano* was paw. I worked and worked with him to no avail.

On occasion, Mama Tere would ask how the lessons were coming. I told her, "Sadly, we got stuck with a monolingual dog."

Then, as if to show differently, she looked at Scotty and said, "*Ven aquí*" and Scotty got up and went. Obviously, he understood her Spanish.

One day I came up with an idea that I thought was brilliant. I told Mama Tere, "I finally taught Scotty a command in Spanish."

I called him over and said, "*Mueve la cola. Mueve la cola* or wag your tail, wag your tail." Scotty wagged and wagged his tail.

Mama Tere laughed and said, "*Eres muy viva, hija.* You are bright, my girl." Pleased with myself I ran off to play.

When Mama Tere's eyesight started to fail, Scotty would step in front of her to keep her from crossing the street when a car was coming. He protected her from other dogs, cats, or anything or anyone that posed a threat. We didn't worry about Mama Tere if Scotty was with her. Most of the dogs in our part of town had names that described them. Names like Spotty, Brownie, Snowball, and *Chiquita* were heard throughout the neighborhood. Whenever you yelled for your dog, three or four showed up running.

These dogs' may have been disposable to others, but they were our companions and protectors. We loved them, and they loved us because we took them in when they were abandoned. For that reason, they were fiercely loyal. With dogs, cultural practices and beliefs emerged. Among those rules was that we couldn't see dogs tied together when the female was in heat or we would develop a *perrilla* a little dog volcano of pus on our eyelid. We also were taught to keep our eyes away when they were taking a dump, or we would get styes.

STYE
FREE
ZONE

Westside San Antonio was declared
a bona fide stye free zone.
So, whenever we saw a dog taking a dump,
We tapped the tip of our tongue with our index finger,
closing our eyes, we traced a cross atop each eyelid.
This keeps you from getting styes.

Our dogs were family. They ate what we ate and shared the
leftovers of the neighborhood outside the house. For Mama Tere,
her dog would be her sight animal and her guide.

SCOTTY, MAMA TERE'S DOG

One time, after a long bike ride through the neighborhood with my friends, we spied two men in brown uniforms sneaking up on my dogs. Each held a long pole with a wire loop attached to the end. Right at that moment, one of the men scooped up Beauty, a small, white fluffy dog, and threw him in a small wire cage. Then, he trapped Scotty, a medium sized Collie with yellow hair and kind eyes and deposited him in another cage. I ran towards them screaming, "Leave my dogs alone."

He turned around and said, "They don't have tags. We have to take them in."

I looked at my friends and, in a chorus, we all yelled at the dog catchers, "What the heck are tags? Where are you taking the dogs?"

While we were pleading with one of the men to release the dogs, the other dumbo-eared man loaded the cages onto the truck alongside a bunch of dogs and cats that loudly barked. They took Beauty and Scotty and our pets whined while making every effort to scratch their way out and to return to their families.

My mother ran outside frantically asking, "*¿Qué pasa? ¿Qué pasa?*" In a calm voice, I told Mama Ruben about the brown uniformed men, the poles, and the truck that raced off with our dogs. That's when she explained all dogs were supposed to get their rabies shots. I asked her if she knew of any dog in our neighborhood who had ever had rabies. She said, "No."

So I said, "That's stupid; why would we want our dogs to get rabies?"

Mother Ruben said, "It's to keep them from getting rabies." Not satisfied with her response, I went to the highest authority and I asked Mama Tere if she had ever heard of a dog in our neighborhood who had ever had rabies. She said, "No."

If dogs in the neighborhood had never had rabies, why did they need a shot?

When my older brothers and sisters came home, I told them what had happened to our dogs in between sobs. They also started crying. They couldn't believe our dogs had been picked up by the dog catchers.

Paul said, "I thought they were smarter than that!" We decided to gather all our money and give it to Papa Mundo and Mama Ruben to spring them out of dog jail.

After rummaging through our drawers, wallets, purses, pant pockets, and sofa cushions, we came up with $6.89. Then, I went to get my piggy bank. Santos, my brother, with a sad look said, "Is that the money you've been saving for that doll and carriage you've been wanting?" I nodded and told him to smash it. The pig contained $12.00 plus change. We gave Papa Mundo the money and begged him to get Beauty and Scotty out. He told us we'd go get the dogs in the morning.

The next day we all woke up early, climbed into our car, and drove to the dog pound. When we arrived, we were told to go look for our dogs. First, we ran into one dog. Then the other. They were in separate cages and looked frightened and appeared disoriented.

With love, we told our dogs we were taking them home. With that news, they jumped up and down, intensified their barks, and in desperation scratched at the wire cages.

While we were comforting our dogs, my parents were speaking to two men. I was watching my parents and could tell they were upset. Then Mama Ruben and Papa Mundo walked up to us and said, "We don't have enough money for both dogs."

I screamed, "What do you mean?"

"One will have to stay." My sisters and I wept, and my parents hugged us, instructing us to decide which one. We cried even harder until we ran out of tears.

My oldest brother said that Scotty was old and that he probably wouldn't live much longer. Everyone agreed.

But I told them, "Scotty has been our dog for eleven years and he has been a good watch dog. Besides, who would walk with Mama Tere when she wanted to visit her friend across the street?" I reminded them "She can't see very well anymore, and we depend on Scotty to keep her safe by stepping in front of her if a car was coming down the road."

My oldest sister Yolanda asked, "So, you vote for Scotty?"

"Of course not, I want them both," I uttered.

My sister Janie said that Beauty was a puppy and was very cute and playful and besides, she always slept with her.

I looked at her and said, "You sneak, I knew you were hiding Beauty in your bed at night. I'm telling!" After an intense discussion, a vote was called for. I refused to vote, but they chose Beauty.

My best friend María was waiting for us and I told her about Scotty.

"At least you were able to save one dog. Most of the time, when my friends' dogs disappear, no one ever goes looking for them and you know what they do to the animals in the pound—they gas them and then feed them to the lions at the zoo."

I started bawling, and my brother Paul put his arm around me saying, "Don't listen to her, she doesn't know nothing; they'll take care of him."

"Are you sure," I asked?

"I think so," he replied.

"Will they give him an ice cream cup every day? You know Mama Tere buys him one during the hot summer months from Mr. Garcia, the *paletero*." My brother told me that he thought they would.

"I'm sure some nice family will come by, look at his cute face, and take him home to live the life of Riley." I had no idea who Riley was, but it sounded wonderful. My only consolation was to wonder what dogs would come to our doorstep, the way Scotty and Beauty showed up. I felt a little better and tried to stop crying; I really did because I didn't want my parents to feel bad, or more awful than they were already feeling. As we walked away with Beauty in my sister Janie's arms, the only thing in my mind was Scotty's sweet, sad face.

PERVERTS IN OUR MIDST

In our neighborhood, dogs weren't the only problems with which we had to contend. Two-legged dogs who preyed on girls also lived in the Westside. On the way to our junior high school, we often saw this dirty old bum of a man. The first time he passed us, he whispered a bunch of obscenities.

Emma asked, "*¿Qué dijo?* What did he say?" Dumbfounded, we joined in the chorus, as we stared at one another.

"What?"

"What?"

"What did he say?" We though he might be a nasty and dangerous man and we made a pact to look out for each other.

"*Mira. Mira.* Over there," I yelled. "Look. Look. He's coming this way." We had agreed cross the street. We sealed our pact with the warning, "Just don't get hit by a car." If he followed us when "he got to the pecan tree in front of Tobar's Icehouse, we would cross back again, and again in a zig zag pattern, until he gave up and went away."

Natalie, whose dream was to become a nun, said "He's not right in his head; we need to pray for him."

Emma, who'd already gotten a degree in street smarts and as one who never held her tongue, blurted out, "Bullshit! *Es un desgraciado*, he's a bastard! I'll pray alright, *que lo machuque un carro*. Pray a car runs over him." Natalie would make the sign of the cross and I would laugh.

Whenever we let our guard down and didn't spot him from a distance, or when we didn't want to play this cat and mouse game, we let him pass by. He would lower his face, and, in a deep, low venomous whisper he said our private body parts in Spanish diminutives such as: *panochitas, nalguitas, chichitas*, as if his use of the diminutive form of "itas" made the verbal and mental assaults less vicious.

Without exception, Emma always yelled out, "*Cabrón*."

I must point out that he never touched our bodies, but he used his words as weapons against us. We avoided him even if it meant stepping onto the street, brushing up against a cyclone fence, or walking in mud or a pile of poop. We were ready to attack him if he tried anything. When we saw him coming, we would pick up the largest stones and the sharpest sticks we could find—with what was available to us we would defend each other. We were nerdy girls— smart and innocent—but also streetwise. You couldn't grow up on the Westside and not learn a thing or two about staying safe. We carried our valor in our bones.

Infrequently, we would take side streets hoping to avoid the perv. Sometimes it worked and sometimes it didn't. We tried not to get off our regular path because we would often confront a pack of dogs daring us to pass. We would have some serious face-offs, but we lost every single time. It was one of those times that Emma instructed us to, "Back up slowly, and quietly run for your lives."

About a block before we got to school, we saw a group of boys hanging out, smoking, drinking, and looking tough because they were. One of them said, "*Al alba, ahí vienen las monjas.* Heads up, here come the nuns." That's what they called us. We broke out in riotous laughter.

As we passed by, I said, "Hey Bopper," in the deepest, coolest voice I could mimic, which came out sounding like that of a high-pitched honking goose. But I quickly recovered and continued, "I've got that paper you asked me to write for you. I'll give it to you during lunch, it's due today." His friends pushed him. Called him *pirujo.* My friends left me and ran for cover. I hitched up my long skirt and ran after them yelling, "Wait for me. Wait." My heart-throbbed and his *camaradas* roared with laughter.

We were late to school, and, of course, Mrs. Brown, the attendance lady, glared at us and warned, "Girls, you need to wake up earlier, so you won't be late. I have to give you all demerits."

Emma, being her usual self, glared right back at her and said, "Ay Miss, we get up early enough," adding, "For your information, Natalie gets up every morning to attend the early mass at Guadalupe Church, with her *Mamacita* and *Abuelita.*" To make a stronger point she added, "Besides with this hot weather no one sleeps in on the Westside. Our tiny houses get too hot, and, to tell you the truth, we wouldn't be late if we could walk in a straight line instead of a big, ole zig zag."

Mrs. Brown looked at us with a puzzled look. She had no clue what Natalie was talking about, and we were not about to tell her.

While we waited for Mrs. Brown to write up our demerits, Emma saw a girl she knew sitting in a corner in the room and walked over to her. The girl was very pretty with big green eyes, but she looked like she had been in a cat fight. She had deep long scratches on both sides of her face.

When Emma returned, I asked "Jesus, what happened to her?" Turns out that last weekend, she had been jumped by the Dots going home from a house party. The Dots didn't scare us, even though we were shaking in our bones. The Dots, a local girl's gang, were tough and mean and our aim was always to stay under their radar.

Emma retorted, "That's why I only hang out with you punks, I mean nuns. The worst thing you do is skip your nightly rosary."

I turned to her and added, "In my class, I have several girls that are Dots and they're okay. Except for this one Dot that never had paper or pencil and she's forever borrowing mine. It would be nice if she would at least say 'Thank you.' Wouldn't you know that the other day when class was over, I asked the Dot to give me back my pencil, telling her, 'I would save it for the next time she needed.' She looked me over, broke the pencil in half, and throwing the pieces at me walked away laughing. All I could say was, 'That's it! I'm finding me another place to sit.'"

Loretta turned to me and said, "Maybe that girl was jumped for batting her false eye lashes at your Bopper, and someone didn't like it."

I replied, "Yeah, Bopper is so dreamy, but he's way out of my league," while thinking to myself "I don't have big boobs," as my brother Paul liked to remind me.

"Teresita you are what boys call a perfect 36, except in your case it's 12, 12, and 12." Geesh, brothers could be brutal.

Mrs. Brown brought me back, when I heard her say, "Git along now. Git, get to class. Git," as she handed out our demerits. We looked at one another, giggled, and galloped off neighing loudly along the quiet hallway.

When we regrouped after school to walk back home, I told my friends, "Hey, chalk one up for flat-chested, plain looking girls. We'll never have to worry about being jumped by the Dots." As I looked at their faces, I quickly back-pedaled and continued, "I mean, we're just late bloomers—well not you Loretta, you blossomed years ago. And we could all look pretty if we spent more than one minute combing our hair and maybe even putting on some make-up, and stuffing our bra with tissues, like many of the girls in school, but obviously not you Loretta, you're already stuffed to the gill. I mean, really, if you ask me, you're all very pretty girls except . . ."

Emma stopped me with, "Tere, zip it." And I did!

Along the way our conflicts as girls were few. As far as the perv, I don't know why we never reported this poor excuse of a man to a parent, our siblings, or a teacher. I think I was the only one who almost broke down and told my mother, but I was afraid she would tell Papa Mundo who would hunt him down like a dog to bash his face in. I didn't want my Papa to get in trouble. I suppose each one of us had our own reason to stay silent.

Except, except one day while walking to school Emma said, "I think he likes Loretta and her large headlights."

Loretta blurted, "Shut up," and then after a while added, "Emma, how's that training bra working out for you?" We laughed.

Then Natalie said, "What a stupid name, training bra. What idiot came up with that?"

A week later Loretta declared, "Starting tomorrow one of my sisters will be driving us to school." I think Emma's comment spooked her and she told her family about our tormentor. And, knowing my Westside, it was just a matter of time before everyone would hear about this predator and justice would be swift. The first line of defense on our side of town was *familia*. We didn't have the luxury of calling the police. We didn't want the *chotas* or cops cruising our neighborhood because that could lead to asking, "*¿Dónde están sus papeles?*" This would result in hard working, honest people packing up and leaving in the cover of night. Besides, we were used to living in the wild, wild west—our beloved Westside.

This skeletal man, dressed in faded, dusty clothes, with a sad, saddle bag face, suddenly vanished. We never saw him again. He faded from our neighborhood but never from our minds.

MY BUS FRIEND: DOÑA CLARA

School had just started. I was running late to catch the first of two city buses to arrive on time for band practice. I kept hoping that David, our regular bus driver, was working this morning. I knew he would wait a few minutes and then just punch it to get back on schedule. David knew all his regular morning passengers and did everything possible to get us to our destination safely and on time.

As I climbed aboard the bus I said, "Thank you David. You just saved me from getting a bunch of demerits. Do you want a potato and egg taco? It's still warm." I fetched it out of my bag.

David smiled and answered, "No I'm good. I just started a new diet, but I'll take one next time."

I laughed and said, "Ah, yes. Those miracle diets."

Before I took a seat, he handed me a white envelope and said, "Hey, here's something else I wrote. Look at it and tell me what you think." The envelope was stamped, "overdue notice" in big red blocked letters. I carefully slipped the envelope inside one of my textbooks and later found poetry written on it. People saw David as a mere bus driver, but he was also a gifted writer. In time on both sides of the border, he became a renowned Mexican song writer and was given numerous awards for his talent.

The bus was crowded, but I carefully searched for Doña Clara whom I most liked to sit next to. However, Richard's broad smile distracted me as I smiled back and waved. My math homework last night had been confusing and I knew Richard was a math whiz who could help me with it, but I continued looking for Doña Clara.

Next, I saw our harmless neighborhood wino going only he knew where. "*Que Dios lo bendiga. ¡Esclavo del alcohol!*" My thought translated my grandmother's voice inside of me "May God bless you. Slave of alcohol!" I pulled out my extra taco for the wino. Before I could say a word, he had snatched it out of my hand and buried it deep inside a large floppy pocket of a tattered coat much too large for his thin frame.

As I moved down the aisle, I saw Señora Martinez. I could've sat with her to get the most recent news on her son's family. But just then, I saw Doña Clara waving and motioning for me to go sit next to her. I rushed there because she had saved me a seat even though the bus was packed like a can of sardines with people all lined up in tight rows. Most of those standing were young and following what they had been taught by giving their seat to the elderly, pregnant women, or women with small children. As the bus lurched forward, it swayed from side to side like a wave in the ocean. People made room for me to pass even while they struggled to maintain their balance, and I carefully made my way to Doña Clara.

When I sat, I pulled out the envelope David had given me and read out loud. After finishing I said to Doña Clara, "Wow, this one is great!" She, and those sitting or standing nearby, clapped. As I exited the bus that morning, I returned the envelope to David and asked him, "Did you hear the clapping back there?" He smiled and I said, "People loved it. Keep writing."

I loved sitting with Doña Clara because she always crocheted on the bus and gave me lessons. She would bring my half-finished, indigo blue scarf tucked away in her bright red large, plastic bag. As my teacher, Doña Clara had an extra needle to guide my fingers one loop at a time. My objective was to finish it by Thanksgiving. Given the uncertainty of our meetings, we were not done. But I was not disappointed because it was going to be a Christmas gift.

By the time of year that crafted red construction paper Santa Clauses with cotton balls mustaches and beards began to appear on the windows, Doña Clara and I finished the scarf. When I got home, I wrapped it in tissue paper, and hid my mother's Christmas surprise deep inside one of my dresser drawers.

Doña Clara and I maintained our bus friendship. I loved listening to her colorful stories and admired that while she had suffered much, she had managed to remain joyful. The week before Christmas, I gifted her a small leather coin purse wrapped in bright crepe paper.

In return, she pulled out a small box from her plastic bag and said, "Es un pequeño regalito. But don't open the gift until after your mother opens the scarf you made for her." On Christmas morning, when we opened gifts, I waited for Mama Ruben to open her scarf. She loved her gift and immediately wrapped it around her neck. Then, I opened Doña Clara's gift. She had given me the exact same scarf. I was thrilled.

"How perfect," I said to myself as I wrapped the scarf around my neck.

Soon enough, I was ready to return to school and looked forward to seeing David, Doña Clara, and my new bus friends and acquaintances. In the bus line I had created a community within my greater Westside. I was part of the 6:30 am morning crew that exchanged greetings, shared homemade tacos and cookies, and watched out for each other. I loved riding the bus.

The first day I returned to school, I wore Doña Clara's scarf; I wanted her to see me wearing it, but she wasn't on the bus. Days went by and the bus passed her usual spot. Several times, I asked David if he had seen Doña Clara.

David said, "I don't think so."

"Gee, David, you're no help," I snapped at him.

"*Chica*, it's hard to keep up with millions of people coming in and out of my bus."

I retorted, "I'm just worried about her."

I never saw Doña Clara again. At first, I imagined that she had left the Westside and moved to a large home with two bathrooms somewhere on the northside. But I wasn't convinced. I didn't know where she lived or worked, otherwise I would've looked for her. As the weeks slowly turned into months, my search ended.

One day, a woman on the bus approached me and asked me if I remembered Doña Clara. I replied, "Yes. Of course, I remember her." She dug inside her purse and pulled out a small package wrapped in white tissue paper.

She handed it to me and said, "She wanted you to have it." I opened it and found my crochet needle. Doña Clara, and other women around me, created the environment for me to become the person I imagined.

COOKING
TOGETHER

At home, the kitchen was my favorite place. While the *mujeres* prepared our meals, I sat at our kitchen table and colored, cut out paper dolls, or practiced my letters and numbers while I watched my mother and grandmother delicately move back and forth.

Years later, I realized I'd been a witness to their dance. A dance between women, working together in small, cramped spaces where they dispensed their love and care. They were,

Walking, thinking, and planning,
looking, reaching, and grabbing,
getting, wiping, drying, and clearing,
setting, cleaning, rinsing, and gutting,
cutting, dicing, and filling,
cooking, boiling, frying, and toasting,
tearing, peeling, crushing, and pounding,
blending, blanching, and sieving,
slicing, chopping, and heating,
bubbling, waiting, and mixing,
rolling, stirring, and watching,

tasting, storing, and zipping,
stooping, starting, and turning,
spinning, gliding, and bumping,
stumbling, passing, and sliding,
pivoting, twisting, and bending,
stopping, resting, and talking,
laughing, gossiping, and cursing,
howling, missing, and recalling,
crying, regretting, and wondering,
questioning, reflecting, and weeping,
remembering, lamenting, and accepting,
resigning, forgiving, searching, and searching
another way to show love.

In our family love came in many forms, not just as food
they cooked. The women in our family also made our attire and
beautified the clothes we wore.

BEADED
SKIRTS

My home was our refuge. There, we learned to cook, sew, and create household projects. One major undertaking was the beading of three folkloric skirts bought for my sisters and me. These beautiful skirts were purchased during one of Mama Ruben's many trips to Mexico to visit relatives, each with a hand-painted scene of original art. I recall Mama had asked us what color skirt we wanted: Yolanda, my oldest sister, insisted on black and white, Janie wanted lime green, and I asked for hot pink. Once she returned and showed us the skirts, she and my grandmother, Mama Tere, set out to hand-bead each one. At our neighborhood community center celebrations and at the yearly school festival at De Zavala Elementary School, we performed with those skirts. No one had more dazzling attire than Mama Ruben's girls.

Long forgotten, one time I stopped in to check on Mama Ruben, and those colorful beaded skirts came to mind. I asked, "Mama, what happened to our beaded skirts?"

Mama Ruben responded, "*Pues, no se.* I don't know." Perhaps I asked the question far too late. I should've asked her before her memory faded.

JANIE AND HER FRIEND BERTHA RODRIGUEZ

I recall we took classes at various places in San Antonio, including the Guadalupe Community Center. Our dance instructor was Señorita Almaguer, the niece to Bertha Almaguer who was the founder of folkloric dancing in San Antonio. We excitedly trailed after her because she was our neighbor and related to our mother's friends. Señorita Almaguer was an exceptional talent, and several of San Antonio's oldest and wealthiest families brought their non-stereotypic Mexican blonde-haired, blue-eyed daughters for lessons. The first time I saw these out of place children I thought, "They must be lost. They don't belong here." A couple of years after, Señorita Almaguer relocated to Spain, joined El Cordova's world-renowned dance troupe, and toured throughout Europe and Japan.

These skirts were our prized possessions. Every time I came home from school, I would see Mama and my grandmother sewing thousands of colorful sequins and beads onto each skirt. Even relatives from Mexico who happened to be visiting and staying with us, and friends and neighbors who would stop by for a quick visit and maybe even indulge in some *pan dulce* and *café*, would automatically pick up a skirt and start attaching sequins. The number of hours spent on each skirt cannot be measured because time was stolen here and there throughout the day, weeks, months, and years, until each skirt had the perfect sparkle. I loved my skirt. When I twirled, it looked like a thousand colorful stars were reaching up to the ceiling to brighten our cozy living room.

When I saw my sister Yolanda, I inquired if she knew where our skirts were stored.

She said, "I have no idea."

I told her, "You know, those skirts held many people's personal secrets, *chisme*, gossip, and even our neighborhood's history."

My sister looked at me and said, "They're just skirts," and added while laughing, "Ay, you and that imagination of yours."

I retorted, "No, I saw Mama Tere and Mama Ruben and all the women who visited laughing, crying, cursing, and shamelessly confessing their sins and indecencies."

Yolanda rolled her eyes, and said, "Well maybe they're hanging in some wealthy person's closet or even on display in a museum." After thinking about this for some time, I decided that I'd rather have the skirts treasured by someone than in a garbage heap. I just hope that whoever has our skirts appreciates them as a labor of love. When I close my eyes and imagine Mama Ruben and my grandmother lost in their work and thoughts, I can even hear Mama Tere's voice lamenting that she'd lost most of her eyesight working on those skirts.

Those skirts hold memories and secrets. These recollections brought me back to my cousin's first marriage to a Canadian woman with whom he fell in love while at the university.

EDUARDO
AND ADA

Trips between both nations were commonplace. We valued those visits from our Mexican relatives to San Antonio. Sometimes they came without announcing themselves, and other times they called to let Mama Ruben know. One day, when my siblings and I came home from school, Mama Ruben told us Tío Jorge was on his way here, and he would be spending the night. Tío Jorge was the *Alcalde* Mayor of Múzquiz, Coahuila, and he was picking up his two sons the following day. His oldest son, Eduardo, who was fifteen years older than me, was arriving from Canada where he was finishing his master's degree at the University of Quebec in Montreal. After that, Tío Jorge was scheduled to pick up Beto in Austin, where he was a junior at the university, and they immediately would drive back to Múzquiz, which was six-hours away.

A few days after my uncle Jorge left, mother received a call from one of my aunts. By the number of "*No lo puedo creer,*" and the litany of "*Pobre Sara,*" I imagined something grave had taken place.

That night I overheard Mama Ruben tell Papa Mundo that Eduardo had gotten a girl pregnant, and he'd decided to marry her. My aunt Sara, Eduardo's mother, was devastated because he was engaged to Isabella, his girlfriend of eight years who came from a good Catholic family—a good, *rich* Catholic family—and they'd planned to be married as soon as Eduardo graduated. They even had finalized some wedding arrangements. Now, my cousin was going to marry his pregnant girlfriend, Ada, a girl he barely knew that he had met at the university in Canada.

After graduating from college, Eduardo and Ada had a small wedding ceremony. Only a handful of college friends and his parents attended. That summer, Eduardo brought his wife to Múzquiz to meet his family. Since Ada was the opposite of Isabella, I wondered what they thought of her.

Born in Germany, Ada and her entire family had been in a concentration camp. No one other than Ada had survived. She was petite and rail thin with short, fine blond hair, beautiful sky blue, intelligent eyes, alabaster skin, and only a trace of light pink lipstick. Isabella, on the other hand, came from a large, boisterous close-knit family. She was tall and curvaceous and had thick, long black hair. Her skin was the color of light caramel and she had large expressive green eyes and wore make-up every day—lots of it—and never went anywhere without her high heels.

My cousin was tall, dark, and handsome. He was intelligent and fun-loving—all of us were in awe of him and wanted to bask in the shade of his shadow. On the other hand, Eduardo's wife appeared aloof and downright cold. We attributed it to her loss of family, to not knowing anyone, and to being from a country where the weather was mostly cold.

At that small municipality of Múzquiz, which was about 100 miles south of Eagle Pass, Texas, Eduardo's family had planned a "small and intimate" reception—there were 200 people in attendance. There, Ada approached my siblings and me to ask, "Who are these people?"

We replied, "Family and friends." She shot us an incredulous glance.

After their reception, Eduardo and Ada moved to California where he landed a plum job with a large corporation that had several offices in South American cities. His bilingual proficiency in Spanish and English cinched the offer. In a few short years, Eduardo became president of the company.

Shortly after their wedding, Eduardo and Ada had a son and the second one soon followed. At the beginning of their marriage, they flew into San Antonio, rented a car, and drove to Múzquiz. After a few years, only Eduardo and his sons visited. Ada would infrequently fly in with them and stay at our house. Eventually, she stopped coming altogether. After their two sons graduated from college, Eduardo and Ada divorced.

At a relative's funeral in Múzquiz, Eduardo ran into Isabella who was widowed. Not even a year later, they secretly met in Las Vegas, Nevada, married, and began their "happily ever after."

Mama Ruben opined, "*Fue el destino que esa pareja se casara.* It was that couple's destiny to marry."

Our Mexican connections are plentiful. It is as if the land in-between joins us rather than separates us from our ancestral past. Either side of the family would freely travel from one nation to the other, and funerals would be but one of the many reasons for their visits.

FAMILY VISITING WITH RELATIVES AT
LAKE *XOCHIMILCO*, MEXICO

MAMA LITA'S PORCH, A LIFE OF ITS OWN

After my mother's death, our maternal *Abuelita* became our Mama Lita, and my brother Jesse went to live with her and Tío Chuy across the street from Our Lady of Guadalupe Church in San Antonio's Westside. We were there so frequently, when the bells tolled, calling people to come, come, come, we witnessed Mama Lita shuffle toward the porch. Her tiny steps belabored with the beat due to her fragile health.

To rest, she sat on the old glider from long-ago and recalled happier times. We sat next to her weary body, reaching for the aging hands she had worked to the bones. We cupped them in our own vibrant hands, and made our best effort to keep her tethered to this place. However, my small, fearful, fluttering heart hinted Mama Lita was getting ready to fly away to a place without time, to an impending death.

We saw people enter OLG from the porch and got a hint of the gold altar deep in the belly of the church as the massive brown plain doors that opened wide like a frozen yawn, attributed only to the unforgiving Texas heat. The church was jam-packed with the bodies of the faithful. Inside, Father Carvajal, in his green robe, started the

Introductory Rites of the mass, and I am reminded that my departed
Mother and her two sisters were *Hijas de María*. That brother
Jesse was an altar boy and attended school in this community. That
the family embraces Catholic virtues, or human virtues, kindness,
respect towards others, sacrifice, and love for humanity.

Surely all is well in the world. All was well in mine. However, my
family and I never knew when a dead body would be in our midst.

UNDERGROUND FUNERAL HOME

"*¿Van a velar muerto?* Are they holding a wake?" I asked. This was the one question I wanted my brother Jesse to answer truthfully when he asked me to spend the weekend with him and our grandmother, Mama Lita.

"No. No," he said.

"*Prométeme* and say cross your heart and stick a needle in my eye," trying to get the truth out of him.

"No. No, *va a haber muerto*."

My grandmother's house was right across the street from Guadalupe Catholic Church, one of the oldest churches in San Antonio's Westside. The house right next door to hers was a small, wooden, white, shot-gun style home. Unlike my grandmother's house that had a nice-sized porch, this house had no porch at all, and the front door almost butted-up to the sidewalk. The houses were side-by-side and were separated by an old, rusty wire-mesh fence that leaned towards my grandmother's yard, as if it was about to die. If the neighbor's window curtains were drawn open, Jesse and I had a view of people walking past the window in various stages of dress which made us laugh. You could hear everything too.

JANIE, TERESA, AND JESSE IN FRONT OF
THE UNDERGROUND FUNERAL HOME

Mama Lita would often say, "*Hasta los pedos se olían* we could even smell their gases."

The house next door to Mama Lita's was also a *funeraria, sin permiso o licencia,* an unlicensed funeral home and every so often, *a velorio,* or wake was held for *muertitos,* in a coffin that sat in the middle of a small living room. There wasn't a sign that welcomed the dead, but people knew that they could bring their departed loved ones to this house. Men, women, and children, mostly dressed in black, would arrive at dusk to congregate on the sidewalk, waiting for the door to open. Later, the crying and wailing began, and the slow, rhythmic-like murmurs of prayers were recited, and the smell of incense floated out of the house and spilled into the street.

A few nights before coming to spend the weekend at Mama Lita's house, my friends and I took turns telling scary stories about *La Llorona, La Lechuza,* and other apparitions—the scarier, the better. In that context, Louie talked about how certain spirits are trapped between earth and the hereafter, and that the spirits showed up at funerals to enter someone's soul.

"*Wachale,* you have to cross yourself and spit on the ground, to keep those evil spirits underneath your feet," he said. I freaked out. Louie didn't know Mama Lita's house was next to a funeral home.

When I arrived at Mama Lita's, my brother told me that there was going to be a *muerto* a dead body at the house next door, after all. He swore up and down that he didn't know. So, that evening we waited for the hearse to arrive, but the *muerto* arrived in a coffin covered with large blankets on the back of an old pickup truck.

No matter how scared my brother Jesse and I felt, we still walked up and down the sidewalk and tried to get a glimpse of the *muertito.* And after telling Jesse what our friend Louie had said about evil spirits and their love of funerals, we crossed ourselves and spit on the ground just in case. Some nights we spit so much that our throats became so parched we could barely speak. Tío Chuy would ask us a question and all we could do was croak.

He would ask, "¿*Qué tienen huercos malcriados?*" Once we were done with our back-and-forth walking and spitting and crossing in no order, we spent the rest of the evening in the front porch with a tall glass of water to watch all the comings and goings until the last person left.

My brother and I suspected that the corpses brought into this funeral house were not embalmed. We asked, "What other reason was there for holding the *velorio* burial that same day?"

Another thing we wondered, "Why was there never a priest inside that *funeraria*? What, with the church being right across the street, and all?"

There were only two bedrooms in my grandmother's house. My uncle, Tío Chuy, a confirmed bachelor who took care of Mama Lita after all her children had died of TB, slept in one room, and my grandmother and brother slept in the other. Whenever I visited, I slept with them. The soft ample bed was up against the window next to the funeral house. Those nights when a corpse was spending the night next door, I made my brother sleep next to the window in case the body suddenly decided to enter the house through the bedroom window. Some nights, the slightest noise would wake us up, and, after swearing we could hear someone digging in the backyard, we would jump out of bed pillows and blankets to Tío Chuy's room, which was on the opposite side of the house, and sleep on the floor. The next day, after having worked into a frenzy with our imaginations during the night, we ran to the backyard to look across the fence for freshly dug graves. We were certain corpses were being buried right under our noses.

When I went back to my Durango Street home, I sat in my favorite kitchen chair while Mama Tere and Mama Ruben were cooking, I told them all about the *funeraria, los muertitos, y el miedo que me entraba.* They burst out laughing.

Mama Tere would say, "*Teresita. No le tengas miedo a los muertos, tenle miedo a los vivos!*"

Before I went outside to play, I said, "Mama Tere *cúrame de susto.*" Mama Tere had been right when she warned us to be careful of those who were alive. This was most evident when we went to Joske's, and I noticed the arrangements for drinking water.

WATER FOUNTAINS AT JOSKE'S

"Get dressed Teresita," Mama Ruben yelled. "As soon as your father gets home from work and eats his breakfast, we're going downtown to the Joske's sale and then we'll go to Solo Serve, if Mama Tere isn't too tired." As soon as she mentioned its name, I made a mental note to drink plenty of water before heading out, because making choices was hard for me. My parents figured out we would be ready to leave right around the time the store opened, as my father, Papa Mundo, who worked the graveyard shift usually got home at 8:30 in the morning.

Once we arrived, we headed straight to the basement which was where we shopped—I never questioned why we always went there. Occasionally, looking for a special dress, Mama ventured to other floors to look for a nicer dress for herself. While Mama was "shopping" or rather "looking" as I called it, because she rarely bought anything, I ran up the stairs to check out the water fountains hoping that the store had installed a Mexican American one.

Traditionally, Joske's had two water fountains located on every floor, including the Mezzanine where the fancy restrooms were located. If I wasn't helping Mama shop, I would usually hang out by the fountains located right by the stairs leading down to the basement. One fountain had a sign that read, "Whites Only" and the other read "Coloreds Only."

Confused, I would stand and stare at the signs on the fountains trying to decide which one to use but never dared to drink from either one. I was afraid if I took a drink someone would run up to me and yell, "STOP. What do you think you're doing?" And then I would be in big trouble. At times, I would hide behind a free-standing counter or rack to see who took a drink out of each fountain. The only ones drinking water were white or black people. Every so often, I would spot a light-skinned Mexican pretending to be white drink out of the "Whites only," while darker complexioned Mexican pretending to be Black, drank out of the one labeled "Coloreds only." I figured they were too thirsty to wait until they got home or didn't care if they got in trouble.

In the meantime, down in the basement of Joske's, Mama Ruben, kept looking for good—no, *great*—bargains.

"Look Teresita aren't these towels nice and soft? They're such a good bargain!" Well of course I thought, we're at the Bargain Basement Semi-Annual Sale, but I just nodded my head and kept my mouth shut.

While we shopped, Papa Mundo disappeared. After about an hour, I spotted him running down the stairs looking for us. When I walked up to him, he was showing off his shoes. He had walked over to Tony's Shoeshine Stand on Houston Street to get a spit-shine special and visit with his friend to hear the latest *chismes* and neighborhood news.

Mama kept examining the towels, putting them down and picking them up, again. So, I said, "I love the colors Mama and our towels are so old." She looked at me and smiled and I could tell she had decided to buy them. After she paid for the towels, Papa Mundo said he was going home to get some shut eye and would see us later. Mama handed him the heavy, bulky bag of towels to take home, so we wouldn't have to lug them on the bus ride home. We then spent another hour checking out the latest dress styles and colors.

Once we left Joske's, we slowly made our way over to Houston Street window shopping along the way to our destination, Solo Serve on Soledad Street. But before we got there, we stopped at my favorite store, The Candy Shop, to watch a taffy pulling machine that reminded me of two wrestling human arms, one pushing out and the other pulling just as mightily. Today's taffy color was a pastel blue. As I stared in wonder, I recalled that the store only brought out taffy colored orange close to Halloween and deep red and green during the Christmas season.

"¿*Quieres* Teresita?" I heard Mama Tere ask.

"No, *no gracias*," I replied. We left the Candy Store, and crisscrossed Houston Street twice, as Mama wanted to inspect every store window, to see the latest fashions in clothes and shoes, especially Carl's and Vogue. We stopped at Burt's and Baker's, two shoe stores, (Big) Kress, which was a popular five and dime retail department store with one of the best lunch counters downtown, Mangels, Three Sisters, and Burns, all young women's stores, and Pincus, a high-end men's shop.

As we walked down Houston Street, Mama Ruben entered two shoe stores and asked if they had certain shoe sizes in bone white while my grandmother and I waited outside. I had just turned eight and I knew Spring was just up the road and around the bend and it was almost that time of the year to get new shoes. Mama

Ruben bought us two pairs each year, black for the fall and Winter and white for the Spring and Summer. I hoped my feet didn't grow between the black and white shoe intervals, but if they did I knew how to slightly curl my toes to make room. Occasionally, one of my sisters passed down their old shoes to me and they were always too big, but I learned to line the inside of the shoe heel with tissues for a slightly tighter fit which kept them from slipping right off my feet as I walked. I knew Mama would buy me a new pair of shoes if I asked, but I never asked. I could see that she was always trying to stretch each dollar as far as it would go. I learned to make do.

A few blocks before we reached St. Mary's Street, I ran up ahead to spend a few minutes admiring and inspecting the elegant and statuesque Hertzberg clock. I had no idea how it got here but I suspected it had sprouted from the bowels of the earth, broke right through the cement sidewalk, and planted itself at this exact corner. I knew it wasn't just the keeper of time, although I did see several people pause, look at the clock and then glance at their watch, frown, or smile, and walk away. I believed this magnificent clock was here to remind us of the importance of time itself and to make every minute count.

As I stood there I heard, "I'm here," "there you are," or "have you been waiting long?" over and over as this was the perfect downtown meeting place. I wondered how many people had met their happily-ever-after or made promises and sealed them with a kiss or had their hearts broken over those dreadful breakup words, "It's not you, it's me" or planned all types of trysts under this clock. Mama Tere's voice jarred me back, telling me to hurry up because it was getting late.

As we continued walking, I told Mama about the endless stories that might've played out under the Hertzberg clock. She laughed and said, "Ay *hija, tu y tus cuentos.* You and your tales." Finally, we arrived at Solo Serve, on Soledad Street, which was quite a distance from Joske's, where Mama purchased several yards of fabric in colors and textures of those dresses, she admired at Joske's, while Mama Tere selected patterns, zippers, and matching thread to make our very special Easter dresses. But before we went home, we visited the Button Shoppe on Losoya Street to pick out buttons. The store was akin to a kaleidoscope, brilliant colors, and luster. Besides the thousands of buttons in all sizes, shapes, and colors, the store also had the best selection of sequins, beads, feathers, ribbons, and lace.

Once Mama was done with her shopping, we walked over to our designated bus stop and stood in line to catch the Prospect Hill bus home. As we entered the bus, I heard the driver say, "Blacks to the back." During this time, black people had to sit in the back of the bus. But Westsiders had no idea where this absurd rule, ordinance, law or perhaps even a "hear ye, hear ye" public square announcement came from, so we ignored it and we all sat wherever there was an empty seat: in the front, in the middle, or in the back. Once the bus driver gave his little spiel, he could care less where anyone sat. Several times, I would hear someone say, "Sit here. There's no room in the back."

Once my mother and grandmother were seated, I walked down the aisle looking for an empty seat and found one at the very back of the bus. As I looked around at this rolling tin can, I saw a busload of bone-tired working men and women longing to get home.

Miraculously, when we stepped out of the bus, Papa Mundo was waiting to take us home. I must say, it really wasn't a miracle. It simply was knowing our routine or having an estimation or a lucky guess. In my heart of hearts, I believed it was ESP, mind reading, telepathy, or intuition between my parents. But as we approached the car, I heard Papa Mundo say, "I've been waiting more than an hour." At that moment I realized it was just plain old-fashioned patience. Whatever it was, I was just happy that we wouldn't have to walk the four blocks from the bus stop to our home at the corner of Rosillo and Durango streets as both Mama and Mama Tere looked exhausted, and I was starved from all the walking and running up and down the stairs. I remembered Mama had told Papa Mundo to put the roast in the oven exactly at 1:00 pm so it would be ready by the time we got home. When she asked him about the roast I saw the slightest twitch in his eyes, and I knew he had forgotten. Just as Mama Ruben was about to start fussing he said, "*Mira mi amor*, let's go eat at the Golden Star, that way no one has to do the dishes after a long day of shopping." Mama smiled and helped Mama Tere into the car and Papa Mundo turned and winked at me.

I often inspected those fountains at Joske's until the signs were gone. Again, I stood off in my hidey-hole and watched all types of people coming up to drink water: white, black, brown, tall, short, skinny, young, and old. And, at last, I went up to one fountain and took a refreshing drink of water, then glided to the other fountain and drank. To my surprise the water tasted the same. I ran down to the basement and found Papa Mundo and told him the water fountains tasted the same, *the same!*

Boisterously he said, "Why wouldn't they taste the same, the water comes out of the same old rusty city pipes." He looked at me and told me, "Just so you know, Joske's isn't the only store that has these types of fountains and signs, other downtown stores have them as well. It's just that your mother likes to come here."

Years later I asked Mama Ruben if she remembered the water fountains at Joske's and she said, "Water fountains? ¿*Cuales* fountains?" I reminded her about the fountains and the signs and how they filled me with anxiety, and she replied, "Ay, *no. Que asco,* how disgusting! Do not ever drink out of public water fountains *hija,* they're full of germs." For Mama Ruben it was not about a person's color or race. Dirt and germs were enough to discourage us from drinking in public water fountains. My concern with water fountains would be allayed by Joske's Fantasyland.

JOSKE'S—SAN ANTONIO'S EXCLUSIVE DEPARTMENT STORE,
COURTESY OF THE UTSA DIGITAL COLLECTION

JOSKE'S
FANTASYLAND

Despite what part of town people lived, Saturdays we'd end up at Joske's. The city became a kaleidoscope of colors and languages, given that San Antonio had several branches of the military whose young recruits went there to flirt. Also, there were language, and a pilot training schools for young men from Middle Eastern and Asian countries who ended up there. As we walked and shopped, foreign languages were bandied about, and nobody told us to speak English. Downtown was a fun experience and Joske's was considered a "must-go" store when everyone shopped downtown, especially when Thanksgiving opened the doors to Christmas.

As soon as our family's traditional Thanksgiving dinner was over, I pestered my parents to take us downtown to see the beautiful Christmas lights and decorations. To the delight of laughing and squealing children and ear-to-ear smiling adults, what made Joske's such a special store for locals were its decorations during the Christmas season. Children weren't the only ones—my entire family looked forward to our yearly trek to downtown to "ooh and aah" the light spectacles. We drove in a car stuffed with all eight of us; three adults in the front seat, and five, sometimes six kids, if my brother

Jesse come with us. Thank goodness it was a short drive to town.

The first thing that greeted us when we arrived at the store was a thirty-foot tall Santa Claus that sat atop the four-storied roof line waving his mechanized arm at the shoppers as they strolled by. All the windows were covered with beautiful displays of Santa, Mrs. Claus, and a dozen busy elves, along with Frosty the Snowman, Rudolph the Reindeer, and friends. There were igloos, and many Christmas trees in various sizes and colors surrounded by white fluffy snow. Inside, the store sparkled in shimmering red, green, and gold colors. If that weren't enough, the fourth floor exhibited a magical wonder.

Fantasyland was an enchanting castle with towers, a snow-covered courtyard, and a drawbridge. It featured 100 mechanical dancing and talking figures who worked in the bakery, candle maker's shop, post office, and toy and sweet shops. Everything kept time to music, including the tree lights. As you exited Fantasyland, children were given a candy cane and a real Santa Claus was available for photographs.

After we left Joske's, we spent time walking around Alamo Plaza, viewing the city's grand Christmas tree, and posing for pictures. Once we got back in our car, Papa Mundo drove down Broadway Street to see the lights in Alamo Heights before heading home. Clearly, this yearly visit to Fantasyland would not be my last. There would be relatives from Mexico who came to shop during the holidays and Joske's was at the top of their list. Often, Mama Ruben and I would go with them.

As for us, we mostly window shopped. At best we could explore gift-giving ideas, which would remain in our imagination, given our limited means.

SPECIAL SUPPER

When it came to feeding extra people who showed up at our dinner table, there was no doubt in my mind that Mama Ruben performed miracles. She never knew when one of my siblings was going to invite a friend who was hanging at our house to eat. Of course, no one ever said no. One way or another, Mama knew how to stretch, stretch, and stretch our meals to feed everyone, just like that old loaves and fishes Bible story. At other times, relatives from Mexico would call from Eagle Pass to say they were on their way for a quick visit. It was then that Mama scrambled to figure out where everyone would sleep.

One or two days before my father got paid, the two bottom kitchen cabinets where we stored our food was empty. Still, with whatever was available, Mama managed to fix a delicious meal and made us believe it was a special dinner.

It was those times that Mama said, "*Tengo una sorpresa, vamos a comer algo muy especial.*"

Since I was around Mama and my grandmother, I was the first to hear the good news and I immediately ran to tell my siblings, "Surprise, we're having one of Mama's special dinners tonight." Everyone ran into the kitchen and asked what it was.

Sometimes she would say, "We're having fluffy pancakes with hot butter and syrup," or "*huevos rancheros*, with fresh homemade salsa and flour tortillas right off the comal," or "*migas*, with strips of corn tortillas lightly fried in oil with chopped onions, tomatoes, salsa, and egg." She happily clapped to signal what was coming. I was the first to do a second to her claps, and before long all would start clapping. Convinced we were going to have the best meal ever, we were ecstatic with the news. Besides working miracles with what we had, Mama brought her experience in our family's restaurants to create the best meals imaginable, and she was an excellent cook to boot. Every meal was delicious, and it included a small serving of salad with fresh vegetables. She loved cabbage, *calabazas*, beets, green beans, cauliflower, and carrots. These vegetables soon became our favorites too.

After we had all left home, I often stopped to check up on my mother and father. One time I asked Mama if she still cooked those "special suppers" for Dad. She roared with laughter and clapping she said, "I haven't thought about those dinners in a long time. Those were days when there was nothing else to eat but eggs or pancakes, I just didn't want to scare anyone." Mother said she always made sure Dad had a good meal so he could maintain his strength for work. After her concern for him, she focused on the children because we were growing and needed nourishment, then Mama Tere because she couldn't let her go to bed hungry. Then, she would eat whatever was left if anything.

With tears in my eyes, I listened and said, "Oh, Mama. I'm so sorry. I had no idea."

She replied, "Why are you sorry?"

I said, "Because the thought of you going to bed hungry hurts me deeply."

FATHER SANTOS, STANDING SECOND FROM LEFT,
AT EL PROGRESO CAFÉ

She looked at me, laughed and offered, "Don't be sad. Look at me; it didn't hurt me to skip a few meals."

I did. I looked at her and saw this beautiful, strong, hardworking woman who had promised to care, guide, and protect us, and gave us her love. But Papa Mundo also had our back.

EDMUNDO GUERRA III: WORLD WAR III

We were surrounded by love and protection in more ways than one. No one ever bothered us. If they did, World War III would land on their *cabezas*! My father's name was Edmundo (Mundo) Guerra, III, which translates to World War III. Because of him, *pachucos* in the neighborhood left us alone, bullies ignored us, and drug dealers never approached us. Well, except for those two unfortunate thugs who were new to the neighborhood and didn't know about WW III.

Papa Mundo had our backs, and everyone on the Westside knew it. Because of his uncompromising and intimidating reputation, and that everyone knew he packed a German Luger, the one he got from his uncle Amador the *curandero*, who got it from Smiley, el *chimuelo* toothless, who gave it to him for curing his mamacita *de un mal*, who got it from his *compadre's* neighbor who stole it from who knows who. The rule in our neighborhood was, "We don't want or need to know." Let me tell you more.

One day, Papa Mundo saw two men approach my two brothers as they walked home from school. When they got home my father asked, "What did those two *payaso* clowns want?"

EDMUNDO GUERRA III, WORLD WAR III

In unison my brothers said, "To sell drugs." No sooner were the words out of their lips that Papa Mundo took off like a bullet after them. When he caught up to them, there was no, "*¿Qué paso? ¿Qué quieres?* Or this is what my kids said. What do you say?" Without the benefit of the doubt, no excuse me, or a pause, he head-butted them — BAM, BAM. One after the other, the ruffians staggered and fell to the ground. Then, one at a time, he helped them up.

"The next time you come close to one of my kids, I swear by God almighty, you'll never get up."

Papa Mundo was the first to admit he was a holy terror growing up. His mother died when he was nine and his father soon remarried. His stepmother, Nieves, was a kind, gentle woman who took good care of him and his five siblings; they all loved her. Apparently, when he lost his own mother something broke inside him. Nonetheless, Papa Mundo learned to become a hard worker. By the age of ten, he was selling newspapers Downtown, on Houston Street, and provided all his earnings to support the family.

One night while we all slept, Papa Mundo snuck out of the house, as he was known to do. Around midnight, he cut across the vacant lot from his house when he heard a loud grunt and smelt sulfur. When Papa Mundo got home, he began turning on every single light inside the house. His father got out of bed, yelling, "*¿Qué tienes? ¿Estás loco?*"

Later, Papa Mundo would tell his father, "I was scared to death because I knew whatever was hiding under the chaparral was unnatural. I ran in terror. When I looked back, I saw a huge, monstrous boar charging at me. I took off like a demon was coming for me."

His father responded, "*Sí.* It was the devil coming after you."

The next day, they went to the vacant lot to inspect it. The sulfur smell still lingered and on the ground were large hoof prints.

This incident somehow settled him down, but Papa Mundo never crossed that vacant lot again.

In his youth, he was a boxer, a good one, but right before he crossed over to professional boxing, he had a bike accident that tore an entire muscle in his right shoulder which put an end to his glory days. Despite the damage to himself, Papa Mundo kept up with his training.

A few years before getting married, Papa Mundo got into a fight and was knifed. That altercation left him with a scar from right above his ear to the corner of his mouth, running down the side of his face. After we were grown, he told us that he looked for that *maldito* son of a gun that knifed him, but he could never find him. In the neighborhood, he sent a message to tell this *méndigo* bad man that Mundo was coming after him. Two years later, Papa Mundo saw the dastardly man walking down the street.

"I threw on the brakes of my car, put it in neutral, and ran after him." The coward crawled under a house, but I took out my gun and shot in his direction until the clip was empty. I didn't know if I'd killed him. However, years later, I was told he was living in Chicago. I'm okay that he didn't die, even though I wanted him to back then," Papa Mundo said.

Even though Papa Mundo could be a bully, he hated bullies. One late evening my family and I were going home from a wedding at Plaza Juarez at La Villita Downtown when we stopped for a red light. Because the car windows were rolled down, we could hear a woman screaming for help. When we turned to see what was happening, we saw a man beating up a woman. In haste, Papa Mundo stopped the car and ran toward the couple, ignoring my mother's pleas to get back in the car and call the police. He didn't listen. Once Papa Mundo got there, he began pummeling the man. When he was done, Papa Mundo told him, "My name is Mundo Guerra and if you ever beat on this woman again, you know who and what's coming after you." That would not be the only time he exercised his sense of justice.

One evening, two young men came to knock on one of our two front doors looking for Santos, my older brother. At the porch, they told him to stop talking to that girl he was seen with, telling my brother to leave her alone. Santos didn't say much. They left.

No sooner had they left that Papa Mundo rushed to the porch from the other front door where he had been listening.

"Are you going to let those *baboso* slobs come to our house and talk to you like that?" My brother shrugged.

Papa Mundo said, "I taught you to box, to defend yourself, to stay safe in these dark, mean streets, especially a *güerinche* near white like you. First thing you know you're walking down Guadalupe Street and some punks think you're a white boy looking for a piece of ass or drugs, o *mas triste*, both. The next thing is that they're jumping your ass. How many hundreds of hours have we spent punching that bag outside so no one messes with you or Paul? You should have told them never to knock on our door again and then you should have given them the one-two combination, a jab followed by a cross punch. You haven't forgotten that have you?"

My brother responded. "No, I haven't forgotten."

"Well, if those *cabrones* sons of goats ever show up at our door and you don't beat the daylights out of them, guess what, I'm going to beat the shit out of them and you."

Papa Mundo walked away, and my brother just shook his head. Papa Mundo was truly a fighter.

He would've loved one of his nephews to box, but they were their father's sons, not his. Like their father, the boys were quiet, passive, and non-confrontational; there was no boxer in them. Santos Sr. was a responsible father. Although infrequently in our lives, he regularly sent money to various household members. Santos had his eye on college, and Paul, well he always said he was a lover, not a fighter, and besides he wasn't going to let anyone mess up his pretty face or his Elvis Presley *copete* duck tail, which he worked on every single morning for at least thirty minutes in our one bathroom before rushing out to school. Paul would say "Boxing? no way! And how can I play guitar if I break my hand."

Whenever Papa Mundo lost his temper, he began cursing non-stop, not at us directly, just cursing; we always let him off. We knew it was stressful for him to hold down two jobs, to support not only his own immediate family, his wife and daughter, but also a mother-in-law who never accepted him because she believed Mama Ruby had married beneath her. Who wouldn't be tired and short of patience? Mama Ruben would let him release steam and often put him in his place. Usually when she became boiling mad, he would become sweet and meek like a lamb. Papa Mundo, WW III, absolutely worshipped my mother, his Sunday girl, as he called her; he would do anything to make her happy, even put up with five children that were not theirs.

The years went by. We grew older, but whenever we faced hard times, we did it together. Papa Mundo taught us that nothing or anyone was more important than *familia*. At first, he provided a roof over our heads and his protection. In time, and to the very end, he gave us his love and we gave him ours. He did his best and encouraged us to do ours, urging us to get an education.

I knew who had raised me, but I had limited knowledge about my maternal history. Although I was raised by my father's kin, I wanted to know more. One day, I set out to learn about them and worked to reclaim my history.

JESUS CAYETANO SOLIS AND DOLORES ALCORTA SOLIS (MAMA LITA)—
TERESA'S MATERNAL GRANDPARENTS

JESÚS M. SOLIS, TÍO CHUY

That day, when I left school, I did not intend to stop by my brother Jesse's house. Nonetheless, I found myself waiting for the Guadalupe bus instead of Prospect Hill. At Guadalupe and Brazos, I exited the bus one-and-a-half blocks to Jesse's house. My uncle Chuy informed me that Jesse was not home, but that he was expected back at any moment. So, my tío and I sat on the porch glider talking and waiting. I took this time to ask questions about which I had been curious for a long time.

I dove right in. "Tío Chuy, why did you remain single? Why didn't you get married?" This had always been a curiosity of mine.

I waited for his response.

I looked at him and my innocent question seemed to have propelled him to another place, another time. As he turned to look at me, I could see that he was struggling to grasp my question, to process what he had just heard. His face puckered up. His bottom teeth covered his upper lip, and his eyes were moist from the tears.

When he gained his composure, in a matter-of-fact tone, Tío Chuy told me his story. I listened attentively. I had been waiting too long.

"I was in love once. She was a schoolteacher and we almost married. We talked about it. The number of children we would have, the names we would give them, and where we would live. Those things that young couples in love discuss when they're imagining spending the rest of their lives together."

Again, his face had a distant look. Not wanting to intrude in the remembrance of his almost wife and married life, I kept quiet. When he glanced in my direction, I said, "Then, why didn't you marry her?" Like the skins of an onion, Tío Chuy peeled the story a layer at time, sharing his guarded memories.

"Let me tell you a story about our family," he said. "First, you should know that you are a ninth generation Tejana and your roots in Texas run as deep as the mighty oaks we have growing 'round us. Our family came with a Spanish expedition in 1718 that included approximately seventy-two people, thirty-five soldiers, and ten families. One of those families included Francisco Hernandez, your mother's eighth great-grandfather. When they arrived, the land was wild and untamed, mostly thick brush. These early settlers and others that came after began to clear the land, built one room *jacales*, planted crops, and established small ranches. Many died from Indian raids, disease, major and minor accidents, and hunger.

"Fast forward to 1788. For serving in his majesty's military for sixteen years and for the shedding of his blood in defense of Spain's lands, your grandfather Carlos Martinez received a land grant of approximately 66,000 acres where he established a ranch named *El Rancho Señor San José*.

"During the time of the American Revolution, Carlos organized and led cattle drives into Louisiana to feed American soldiers fighting the British along the Gulf Coast under the command of General Bernardo de Galvez. Over the years, the land was lost, some bartered it, others gambled it away, traded it, abandoned it, and good chunks were outright stolen.

"We were living on our ranch, a small parcel of land from the original land grant, not far from San Antonio. While conducting business at other ranches and towns, my father Pablo heard about an outbreak of a deadly disease in many of the ranches and trading posts. At first, clusters of disease were far away, in neighboring states, 'nothing to worry about' people said. As time went by, the outbreak, which now was called consumption, was getting closer, and my parents decided to sell what was left of the family land and move to safety — to San Antonio, near doctors and hospitals.

"We bought a lot across the street from Our Lady of Guadalupe on El Paso Street and built a home. My father's initials are engraved on the concrete curb. He also purchased lots/houses down the street as an investment. However, the Depression hit and one-by-one, he sold his properties to keep the family afloat.

"It wasn't too long that consumption hit us, it would now be called tuberculosis. The illness that drove us to San Antonio came knocking on our door. No matter what precautions we took, staying away from others, shutting ourselves in our home, despite lining the front and back doors with towels, pillows, and rags, tuberculosis snuck in through the cracks in the wood, the roof's shingles, and windows. An invisible, silent, and odorless executioner slipped into our humble home, uninvited and unannounced, and began the decimation of our Tejano family.

"Within a few years, my parents lost four children to this pestilence: Pablo and Donaciano and Manuela and Lilia; all were in the prime of their lives. Your mother who was engaged to be married was spared, at least a few more years." And, he continued, "There was so much sickness, death, and responsibility engulfing me that I terminated the engagement.

"My younger sister Lilia was also engaged to be married to a fine young man in medical school. To save Lilia, my parents visited several ranching families they had been close to and asked if their daughter could live with them until she married, or the epidemic passed. 'We'll pay for her room and board,' they said. Their offer was declined. Lilia passed away and was buried in her wedding gown, along with her dreams of endless possibilities."

When Tío Chuy told me this story, I thought, "The people that declined handed her a death sentence, then?"

He replied, "No, no Teresita," adding, "Those were terrible times, everyone was scared, and they were making every effort to be protective of their family, just like us. It was not a time for finger pointing, judging, or recrimination. Everyone was hiding and running from this disease, just trying to stay alive. Death from tuberculosis was a miserable, horrible way to die."

"Why were you the ones who took care of everyone and everything, what about my grandparents?" I asked.

Tío Chuy replied, "I was the oldest and I was healthy. My parents were beaten down, they could only manage one thing."

"What was that?" After a few minutes, Tío Chuy took a deep breath, and in a whispering voice, he recollected.

"After one of my siblings died and while everyone slept, or pretended to be asleep, I would quietly go around the house, gathering all their belongings and placing them in their bedding. I would carry their worldly possessions outside to burn. Everything. All into the fire. There were times I was tempted to squirrel something of theirs away, as a reminder of their lives, but in the end, I threw it all in the fire. I couldn't take a chance that these keepsakes would spread the disease to the rest of us. I don't know why that plague didn't touch me. But someone had to take care of the comforting and the burying and the consoling. *Dios mío*, those were God awful times! The epidemic ravaged my family. It caused indescribable pain and suffering and shattered hearts. My parents never recovered from the loss."

Tío Chuy's story left me speechless. I had no idea that my questions to him would stir such sad memories. Foolishly, I thought he was going to tell me that one or the other had met someone else that swept them off their feet.

A few contemplative minutes later, Jesse arrived. We chatted about a couple of house parties that were coming up. After a while, he said, "Come on, I'll walk you halfway home." A practice we had carried out since we were children. He met me halfway and we would walk home together.

Tío Chuy was my siblings and my lifelong connection to our mother and her family, there was no one else. He always kept our mother present in our lives through the stories he would weave about his siblings, parents, and life on the ranch. After our *plática* I often wondered how it was possible for him to laugh, love and enjoy life, but he did. He was a shining example of that unconquerable human spirit about which one reads. My mother's brother walked us through a path of reconciliation and took us to a place of peace and joy.

As the years rushed by, I would think about Tío Chuy's story shared when I was in my teens, and often wondered how much of it was factual. It would be many decades later that my brother as he was studying our genealogy concluded that Tío Chuy's story was as he had recounted it. When Tío Chuy told us, "You are Texas hidden history," he was right. Our history would be something that inspired me to thrive, whether in formal education or in daily life. There would be many options ahead for me to learn about the wonders of life. Those lessons were best imparted from my dear beloved parents by choice. I might've not been their blood child, but they raised me as if I were their very own.

BARTERING,
A WAY OF LIFE

Life is as unpredictable as the weather, and the climate and life in Texas is example of this. When it got too hot, Mama Ruben reminded me, "Es la canícula, hija. ¿Cómo se dice en inglés? The dog days of summer." Our state was in the grip of an unbearable heatwave, and I was complaining about having to walk a mere four blocks to catch my first bus to my night class at San Antonio College. Lucky for me, my transfer left me right in front of school.

When I finally arrived, sweaty, sticky, and most likely stinky, I walked into my Economics class and plopped down on a chair. I glanced around and noticed two new students. There were now twenty of us, sixteen white males, four women, and I was one of two Mexican Americans in class. The white males were young soldiers stationed in one of several military bases in San Antonio.

A few minutes after the bell rang, Mr. Hildebrand, my professor, tossed out the word "barter," asking someone to define it. No sooner had he asked the question when several hands shot straight up and began flapping in the air. My hand remained on my desk tightly clasping my pen. Those he called on provided word-for-word Webster definitions.

"I know that word," I thought. Not the word itself, but the nitty-gritty of it; the heart of it. Mr. Hildebrand then asked for examples of bartering and again several hands shot up. My hand remained tightly curled around my textbook.

Mr. Hildebrand's explanation made me think of my neighborhood in the heart of San Antonio's Westside and how bartering was our survival. His words made me think of Mrs. Lozano, our neighbor who cut and permed our hair, and, in return, my mother altered her sons' jeans. And Charlie, whom we knew as *Chale*, my brother's friend, was the only one who owned a suit and would lend it out to friends for special occasions, especially weddings, graduations, and funerals. In return, those same friends were always ready to fix his car whenever it broke down.

Mr. Hildebrand's definition brought back memories of grandmother, *Doña* Tere, who treated people for "*susto*," along with fears, anxiety, and depression. The people she treated bartered with plants, home-grown vegetables, home-made *tamales* and *empanadas*, fresh eggs, and even live chickens.

"Miss Villarreal. Miss Villarreal, can you give us an example?" I heard Mr. Hildebrand ask. I was in shock that he called on me. After all, I was seated toward the back of the class, in the shadow of the student sitting in front, and I certainly didn't raise my hand.

"Don't call on me," I thought. I'm not even supposed to be here; I slid into this school by mistake. After all, not once in my four years of high school did someone ask me if I wanted to go to college and someone, I don't know who, though my friend Jackie swears it had to be the counselor, kept signing me up for secretarial classes and that's where I'll be tomorrow morning, sitting behind a desk translating shorthand notes, typing, and fetching coffee." This is what ran through my mind, as I stared at Mr. Hildebrand.

"Mr. Hildebrand. I didn't raise my hand," I foolishly said. I immediately regretted letting the words stumble out of my mouth and wanting to slap each word down like those pesky mosquitoes buzzing around your ears at night, or yet still, calling back each word and stuffing it in my mouth to swallow them one-by-one, or as a string, the faster the better. But the words already circulated in the air, floating inside each students' ears. A low muffled laughter invaded us, nearly choking his words.

"I know that, but do you have an example?" He responded. "Just, one example."

I looked at Mr. Hildebrand acutely aware of my racing heart, sweaty palms, as a deep red color slowly crept up my face and settled at the top of my small ears. I sat there, staring at Mr. Hildebrand, as I stammered and stuttered, searching for an example, except the words remained stuck inside the roof of my mouth, way up high.

I finally managed to say, "Uh. Uh. No, sir. I can't think of anything right now."

But I could've told him about Miss Lozano, *Chale*, *Mama Tere*, and so many others, if I'd been brave enough, rather than like such an outsider, which was a ridiculous thought given that most of the students had recently stepped on Texas soil, and here I was without a word to say, a ninth generation *Tejana*, according to *Tío Chuy*.

Mr. Hildebrand looked at me and said, "Miss Villarreal. Surely you can think of one example. Just one?"

"*Otra vez*. Again." I thought, "Call on one of the many waving hands dying to show how smart they are." I'll do the work. I'll turn in the assignments. I'll pass your tests. Just don't call on me." I was trying to amass enough hours to get a small promotion at work. All I wanted was to replace the window screens in our home, especially the ones with large holes to keep out God's flying creatures that came in at night to torment us.

Right at that moment the bell rang. I looked up and whispered, "Thank you, *Mama Tere.*" I bolted out of my seat, racing, racing like a lithe mustang to catch the bus home. Good thing I seldom walked at night; it was at this time that the stray spirits and lost souls came out. Sometimes they came into view as people from our past.

SAC–
SAN ANTONIO
COLLEGE

One week after I graduated from high school, I began working as a cashier in the pet department at Neisner's, a five and dime department store downtown. My first paycheck was stolen out of my purse as I walked to the bus stop. Because of this thievery, I found myself with barely enough money to pay for bus fare, much less food to eat. With my second paycheck, I began to save my wages to invest in some badly needed home repairs, such as replacing torn window screens, painting the outside of the house, and installing new linoleum flooring in the kitchen.

During my four years of high school, I never saw or spoke to a counselor. At the beginning of each school year, I found myself in primarily business type classes: typing, shorthand, bookkeeping, business machines, business math, and business English. No one ever asked me if being a secretary was what I wanted, much less, "What are you interested in?"

Except, except for my typing teacher, Mrs. Minnie Rodriguez. She pulled me aside one day and said, "Teresa. You're very smart. You should look into college."

I remember listening to certain students talking about colleges and about the difficulty of their advanced English and Math classes.

I wasn't in those classes. That told me I wasn't expected to go to college. However, I was just as smart or more so I quietly told myself, "If they can go to college, I can too."

And so here I was sitting in an evening speech class at San Antonio College thinking "What the hell am I doing here?" As I looked around, I saw mostly young, white males and none seemed friendly. Right after the bell rang, I saw Albert, one of my brother's friends from the neighborhood. During our break, I walked over to him and told him I was Jesse's sister and took a seat next to him. A few minutes before class ended, professor Barniby told us to be ready to present a ten-minute speech the next time we met.

I worked on my speech all week long and prepared note cards. I recited it so often that I memorized it. When I returned to class, Mr. Barniby asked, "Any volunteers tonight?" There were several people who volunteered, and they got up to speak. Eventually, all but Albert and I volunteered. The instructor called my name and I walked up to the podium. I was terrified. I had never spoken in front of people, especially majority white people. Right before I began to recite my speech, I acted like I was rearranging my notes silently praying, "Lord do not let me make a total ass of myself in front of all these people." I spewed out my speech and practically ran back to my seat imagining I was as red as the pomegranates growing in our back yard. Mr. Barniby thanked me and told me I had done a good job and then called on Albert.

Albert, dressed in his starched long sleeve shirt, khaki pants, and spit-shined tangerine shoes went up to the podium looking *chulo* cute. I don't remember what he talked about, I only remember how everything about him was shaking, his legs, his head, his hands, and his voice. I kept staring at him, smiling, and nodding my head yes to show my support. But it was incredibly painful to watch. By now his face was bright crimson red, like a bad sunburn. Tiny beads of sweat ran down both sides of his face, but he powered through his presentation until he was done.

For a few seconds afterwards, the room was strangely quiet, no one moved, no one spoke, no one breathed. And then, the most incredible thing happened. Simultaneously, as if on cue, everyone jumped out of their seats, whooping, and hollering, clapping, and whistling for Albert. It was awesome and unbelievable, all at the same time. Albert walked off with a huge wide grin and I thought, "Wow! There really isn't a difference between us, we're just as good as they are."

On our last day of class, I inquired. "Albert, what classes are you taking next semester?"

He said, "Vietnam 101. I got drafted."

I was shaken and told him, "Maybe you'll luck out and get sent to Germany like my brother Jesse."

"Maybe," he replied.

Many years later, I ran into Albert at the mall. There we took time to fill in the blank pages of our lives. He had done two tours in Vietnam, used his VA benefits to get a PhD in Literature, and was a professor at a Utah university. I asked him, "Do you ever think about that dreadful speech class we took at SAC?"

We both burst out laughing and he said, "After that class, Vietnam was a walk in the park." With a tight hug, which Mexicans freely give each other, we wished each other well, and walked away. I never saw Albert again, but I purchased one of several books he published about Vietnam.

His presence made me wonder if Albert ever had a nickname. Maybe he was one of those who were saved when he went to war. As I look back, there were many ways to identify oneself when living in the Westside, not only through endearments, but also through diminutive forms of our name, or because of our characteristics and attributes.

NICKNAMES
Y MÁS

Growing up with two sisters and three brothers meant friends were always knocking at our door looking for one of my siblings.

One day, Santos, Janie, and me were watching TV when we heard a knock. Santos answered it and two young men asked, "Hey *Güero*, looking good man; I'm looking for *Bola*, is he here?

Santos said, "No, Peanut. He just left with Smiley and Turtle. They're going over to the school yard to shoot some hoops." When they left, I asked why the boys in the neighborhood had stupid nicknames.

"You're *Güero* because you're light-complected, Paul is *Bola* because he always carries that dumb basketball with him, and Jesse, although he's the opposite of Hercules, is given the name because he's so skinny."

Santos laughed and said, "You're right, everyone has a nickname." He continued, "Come to think of it, I have friends whose names I don't even know; I only know their nicknames. But I think it's better to come up with your own nickname, instead of leaving it up to your friends; that's why I'm *Güero*."

On the Westside, nicknames were another rite of passage.
A way to mark your identity.

Clavo Nail, Smiley, *Changuito* Monkey,
Snoopy, Mighty Rat, *Foco Light Bulb*,
Zap, *Borrado* Erased, *Pelón* Baldy, Goosy,
Red, Birdie, Thumper, Cookie,
Lulu, Beaver, Bopper,
Turtle, *Perra* Dog, Bean, and Puma

These were but a few of the self-assigned nicknames most boys
and girls were proud to claim. Most appeared to embrace these
identities with comfort and love.

Besides these outrageous names, many were given shortened
names as endearments, such,

Frank *Pancho*, Jesse *Chuy*, and *Nacho* Ignacio,
Roberto *Beto*, Jose *Pepe*, and Arthur *Tutti*,
Fernando *Nando*, Charles *Chale*,
Hortencia *Tencha*, Margarita *Mague*, and Connie *Concha*,
Isabella Bela Isa, Carolina *Caro*, and Alejandra *Ale Alex*.

Even though we had our own nicknames, in my family we were
named after relatives and not so immediate relations. My oldest
brother Santos carried my father's name; my brother Paul, was
named after our maternal grandfather; and my youngest brother
Jesse, after our maternal uncle. My sister is named after our mother,
and I proudly carry my paternal grandmother's name.

Santos detested his name because none of his teachers,
professors or bosses correctly pronounced it. He swore to never,

GÜERO AND *BOLA*

ever, name his son Santos. Yet, he called him Santos. And, this tradition continues, all my brothers named their sons after themselves, but the women went against this practice, with names such as Cassandra, Brenda, Lucinda, Deborah, and Lauren.

Also, I had friends who were born on a particular Saint's Day. They were Guadalupe, Ann, Thomas, José, and so on. I often wondered about those unfortunate kids with names like Antibes, Fingar, or Enoch. Then there were those names that made one wonder, "Good grief!" What were people thinking, when someone gave someone else the name Blanca when she was a dark-complexioned child, or Rosa for someone who looked less like the flower and more like the thorns? Then, there was *Dulce* who wasn't sweet at all but carried a cloud of sour disposition, or Chastity who often was the neighborhood's easy girl.

There were those whose nicknames were the exact opposite of their personal traits, such as calling skinny boys Hercules, Beast, or Bear; naming slow deliberate people Rabbit, Speedy or *Flecha*; and calling tall ones *Chore* or Shorty. The worst were those attached to physical appearances: *Perico* was a parrot nose, Rabbit a buck-toothed kid, Dumbo big-eared kid, or *Palillo* a toothpick skinny one, Stumpy for short, *Bola* for fat, and *Chino* for someone with slanted eyes or curly hair. There were nicknames used to show affection: *Gordo* or *Gorda* signifying a fat man or woman, *Flaca* or *Flaco* denoting skinny ones, *Güera* or *Güero* marking a light complexion, and *Prieta* or *Prieto* darker complexion. However, we knew better than to use them in public, unless they were family or a close friend.

Nicknames were an absurdity. In my part of town, they had no malice attached to them. Through them we liked to laugh at each other and ourselves. We developed a thick skin which became invaluable as we ventured into the world. No matter what, those who knew us by our nicknames would always have our backs.

Many years later I ran into a friend from high school who introduced me to her husband. While visiting with them, the husband said he'd graduated from Lanier High School. Then, I asked, "Maybe you know my youngest brother, Jesse Villarreal."

He contemplated the possibility and said, "No. I don't recall anyone by that name."

I responded, "Oh, he always uses Jesse O."

But again he said, "No."

It was only when I said, "Hercules," he smiled broadly

"I knew Hercules. We were best friends."

In our Mexican American communities, nicknames are universal. For example, my best friend Libby from Taos, New Mexico, told me about the time a friend of hers in junior high school stole the basketball, and ran toward the opposing team's side to score. Forevermore, he became known as, "Wrong way."

In the barrio, those nicknames stay with you for life. Nicknames can be fun, but they also can cause pain. The chamberlain who escorted me for the *quince*, regardless of what he was called, didn't have a nickname.

BABY GÜERO AND TÍA MANUELA AT MAMA LITA'S HOUSE,
IN FRONT OF GUADALUPE CHURCH

QUINCEAÑERA

In the small bedroom, the one with an accordion door separating
the kitchen and the room that I shared with my grandmother, Mama
Tere, I was reading in bed and sort of listening to mother who was
tethered to the phone on the kitchen wall, talking to her good friend
Frances about her daughter's upcoming debut as a *quinceañera*.
Many conversations over the past year had transpired, beginning
with the color of the dresses, the procurement of the most sought-
after, impossible to book Mistress of Ceremony from Monterrey,
the various teas that would be held before the event, the upcoming
dance rehearsals for the attendants and their chamberlains, and the
news that her husband's orchestra would be playing.

My sister Janie was one of the *madrinas*. Of course, Frances
wanted to keep Mama apprised of every minute detail. After fifteen
minutes into the conversation, I walked outside, jumped on my bike,
and went to Bazan Library on Buena Vista to return books and check
out new ones.

The following morning Mama Ruben said, "Teresita we have
to go downtown today to buy you *tacones colorados* red high
heeled shoes."

I said, "*¿Por qué?*"

She responded, "*Para la quinceañera.*"

"*La quinceañera*, the one Janie is going to be in?" "*Pos, si. Pero, no.* Instead, she wants to run for Queen of the *Orquidia* Social Club, and Frances hasn't been able to find anyone to take her place. So, you're it. Hurry up, get dressed, and comb your hair. Your *madrina*, Estella, insisted on paying for your shoes, so we're going to buy you some brand-new ones."

My *madrina* Stella and my mother were like peas in a pod. My *padrino* Gilbert had a successful business Downtown—*Guadalupe's Place*—and my *madrina* was very generous with us, buying us clothes for special occasions, bringing groceries, buying Mama Tere new eyeglasses, and helping with other necessities. Mama would often tell her that she didn't need to be spending money on us, but *madrina* ignored Mama, and, of course, we all loved her.

"Mama, I don't want to be in anyone's *quince*. Besides, I don't know any boy I can ask to be my partner."

She replied, "Frances took care of that. She found you an escort, *un joven muy simpatico* a very handsome young man."

I continued, "You know I can't walk in *tacón* high heels. I have enough trouble staying up-right in flat heeled shoes."

"Don't worry, we'll get you a pair of shoes with sensible heels."

"Mama, the words high heels and sensible are *ilógico*."

"No seas *difícil*. Go get dressed and comb that hair of yours."

I told her, "I did comb my hair."

And she said, "*Pues*, then, comb it again."

Off we went on the bus, to find me red high heels, but not too high.

Every time we would walk into a shoe store, Mama would pick up a pair of red high, high heels, longingly admiring them, then she'd looked at me and placed them back. However, her mental picture of me walking in them and falling flat on my face didn't stop her from looking, and I would slap the front of my hand to the palm of the other hand, to mimic me falling forward, and she would walk away from those high *tacones*. We finally agreed on a pair of shoes with a small practical heel.

A few nights later, I went to a dance rehearsal for all the attendants and their escorts. Except my escort was a no-show because he was working. Doña Frances came up to me and said, "Don't worry. Just learn the routine. Your escort will know what to do." There were fourteen couples practicing together and me, dancing with a phantom; I felt humiliated. For distraction, for placing me into this predicament, I kept thinking of ways to murder my sister Janie and getting away with it. Two more rehearsals were scheduled before the *quince* and both times I danced with my ghost. Attendants would look at me with big sorrowful eyes. I smiled and held my head high, as Mama Tere reminded me. Again, my mind would go into overdrive, imagining ways to do away with my sister.

The big event arrived. That morning my sister Yolanda dropped me off at Mrs. Guerrero's beauty shop located behind her house. The beautician combed my hair in cascading curls. At home, Yolanda helped me with my makeup, and I waited patiently for my chamberlain and his parents or older brother to pick me up. I wore Sunday church clothes because the entire débutante party would share a formal meal.

At the designated hour, not one minute before or one minute after, my escort arrived. When he got off the car, I noticed he was driving, not his mother, or father, or an older brother. I couldn't believe my good luck. As I looked at him walking up to my house,

PAPA MUNDO AND PADRINO GILBERT LEANING ON THE JUKEBOX
AT GUADALUPE'S PLACE

Prince Charming soon came-a-knocking at our door, asking for me. Me! He was tall, with light brown hair, and green eyes. When I opened the door to my house, he said, "You must be Teresa. I'm Andres and I am your escort for the night."

Once we were in his car, we chit-chatted about nothing and everything. He talked about how we each knew the Garcias and if I was excited to be part of the *quinceañera* of the year, in our Mexican American community. I told him I had been looking forward to it for the past year and immediately wondered if my nose had grown longer.

Soon, he asked, "How old are you, Teresa?"

I responded, "Almost fourteen."

He said, "What a coincidence, my youngest sister is thirteen, too."

I thought, "Busted!"

My prince charming was attentive, with impeccable manners, and I was in heaven.

At the hall, I noticed a good number of the attendants staring at us in disbelief. Girls who had not been particularly nice to me when we were rehearsing our dance, me with my ghost, I well-manneredly introduced them to Andres. My thirteen or almost fourteen-year-old self, wanted to stick my tongue out at them, but I didn't. The escorts stared at him since, he was older and debonair; even they were in awe of him.

We ate, dressed in our formal attire, took pictures, drove to San Fernando Cathedral for mass where the archbishop blessed the *débutante* and her parents. Then we drove to La Villita for the reception and dance. My chamberlain never took his eyes off me, opened the car door, tucked in my big dress, opened, and closed the door, and put out his arm for me to lean unto. He made me laugh. Made me feel special, I felt like a princess. At the reception, after a delicious meal, we lined up for introductions. First the court, then the *débutante*'s parents and then Raquel the *quinceañera*. It was truly a dream. Every detail was perfect, the table arrangements, the flowers, the decorations, the food, the program, the Master of Ceremony, and the orchestra—her wish had come true.

After we performed the choreographed dance, Andres escorted me to my table where my family was sitting and said, "It's been an honor to be your escort." As he said that, I heard someone calling his name. We both turned around and this beautiful young woman came walking toward him, his girlfriend. I hated her. After introductions and a few nice words, they walked away. I pictured them riding away in a shiny gilded carriage.

I sat down and started to sulk except that my cousin Rosemary made me laugh. Before long, I started to enjoy myself. When my brother Paul arrived, the fun truly began. He was the life of any party, and no one was a better dancer.

He came through for me when he said, "Come on little sister, let's show them how to dance." And we did, or rather he did. After, he danced with Yolanda even though she had brought her du-jour-boyfriend. She was gorgeous and boyfriends were forever rotating in her orbit. Paul danced with Mama and even danced a waltz with Mama Tere. After staying awhile, my brother left to the social club event to cheer for Janie.

At breakfast, the following morning we couldn't stop talking about the night before. Janie wasn't crowned Queen but both she and my brother Paul agreed she had performed a perfect curtsy. As they recalled it, after walking around the entire dance hall, in her thirty yards of silk organza dress, Janie came up to the judges and lowering herself, she bent her upper body, dropping her head all the way to the floor.

"It was perfect," she said. According to Janie, her backless dress was the most striking one of the nights; it was sown by Tía Juanita, the most gifted seamstress in town. Of course, my mother reminded Janie to call her Tía to let her know that the dress had been greatly admired and to thank her for having designed it for her.

After that conversation ended, my sister Janie turned to me asking, "Teresita did you enjoy the *quinceañera*?"

I said, "That would be a yes with a capital YES." Everyone laughed.

Several years later, I went shopping at several stores on Houston Street Downtown for the perfect pair of red high heeled shoes, it was there I found the perfect pair. There, with the shoe in my hand, I heard a man's voice behind me say, "You have excellent taste. Would you like to try them?" In front me of was my chamberlain of years gone by.

I told him "Yes, I'd like a size eight." He returned with a shoe box, took out the shoes, and slipped the right one on my foot. I thought, "Just like Cinderella." Then, he slipped on the left one. I got up and walked around, and turning around I told him, "They're perfect. I'll take them."

When he placed the shoes in the box, he looked up at me, and I asked, "You don't remember me?"

He replied, "Do I know you?" I reminded him about the *quinceañera* of long ago.

"Is that you? You're beautiful. How old are you now?"

I answered, "Eighteen."

He said, "You're gorgeous. I would've never recognized you."

Embarrassed, I felt myself flushing. But I simply said, "Thank you." I notice he was wearing a wedding band.

Had he married the girl he was with the night of the party?, I wondered.

174

I paid for the shoes, he handed me the package, and walked me to the door. Before I left, I said, "I appreciated the way you acted the night of that *quince*. You were gracious, attentive, nice, and you made me feel special; I felt like a princess. I've never forgotten and I'm glad to be able to thank you."

He replied, "Wow! Thank you. That makes me feel good."

We said goodbye and he added, "Stop by and say 'hi' whenever you're Downtown."

A couple of times, when I was downtown shopping, I walked by the store. He was always busy, and I kept on walking. In time, he was no longer there. Good thing. There were other things to keep me busy, such as getting ready for our Good Friday dinner.

GOOD FRIDAY CAPIROTADA

Today was a very special day for our family—it was Good Friday. Mama Tere woke up earlier than usual as she wanted to prepare our home for this holy day. When I heard her getting dressed, I got up and got myself ready. When she saw I was up, she told me to go disconnect the TV, collect all radios and the telephone, and bring them to her.

As I went about my chores, Mama Tere began to cover all the mirrors with black cloth, and I asked, "Mama Tere, why are you covering the mirrors?"

She replied, "To remind us not to be vain or prideful."

In our home, Good Friday was a day of reflection and mourning because of Jesus's crucifixion. In addition to not watching TV, listening to the radio or using the phone, we were not allowed to have friends over. This was the hardest sacrifice, because we could have several friends stopping by to visit at any time.

My mother and grandmother spent most of the day preparing our Good Friday meal, which had to include seven items, no more and no less; it would include *tortas de pescado fresco* or fresh fish patties, *tortas de camarón* or shrimp patties, *nopalitos* cacti, *lentejas* lentils, *puré de papas* or mashed potatoes, *ensalada* salad, and *capirotada* bread pudding.

My siblings and I straightened out the house, helped prep, washed dishes, and set the table. And even though my older siblings were not happy with not talking to or seeing their friends, we all were able to reminisce, laugh, but not too loud, and spend real family time together.

The highlight of the meal was *capirotada* or bread pudding, a special dish that is prepared with day-old bread, in many Mexican American homes on Good Friday. It is also served in Mexican restaurants during the Lenten Season.

As Mama Tere began gathering all the ingredients, we sat at the table watching and learning to make it. It included day-old bread, *piloncillo* (brown raw sugar), cloves, cinnamon sticks, anise, cheddar cheese, raisins, and pecans. There are multiple variations of *capirotada*; some recipes call for bananas and others hold the raisins and pecans.

Right before Mama Tere began to prepare this "*postre bendito* or holy dessert," she bowed her head and said a prayer. Then she began to prepare the dish, explaining that the bread represents the Body of Christ, the syrup the Blood of Christ, the cloves or *clavos* symbolize the nails with which he was crucified, the cinnamon sticks the Wooden cross, and the cheese stood for the Shroud of Christ. When the *capirotada* was prepared, Mama Ruben placed it in the oven. When the cheese had melted, she took it out of the oven, and placed it at the center of our dining table. Mama Tere then called out, "*Vengan todos a compartir.* Come and partake." But even in those holidays, we would hear about sayings that illuminated our path, providing insight with *dichos* and *moralejas* or moral tales about everyday life.

DICHOS Y HECHOS

My siblings and I were raised on *dicho* sayings. My mother and grandmother relied on those few words of sound advice, to remind us about who we were, how we were raised, and about the expectations they had for us. They hoped these words of wisdom would keep us safe and out of trouble.

My mother said, "*Mejor un loco, que dos! Dime con quién andas y te dire quién eres.* It's best to have a crazy one and not two. Tell me whom you run with, and I'll tell you who you are." And, when Mama Ruben found out who Polo's new friend's father was, she exclaimed, "*Que bonito. Hijo de tigere, pintito,*" which actually had nothing to do with niceness but more like Holy Shit! Like father, like son.

When my sister Yolanda was getting serious with a young man who lived out-of-town, Mama would tell her, "*Cuando lejos de ojos, tan lejos del corazón,* or when away from your eyes, away from your heart" and if that didn't work, she would throw out, "*Amor de lejos, amor de pendejos!* Love from afar is a fools love." Another one that she would frequently hurl was "*Vale mas quedada, que mal casada,* it's best to remain unmarried than badly married," and I would think, "Gee Mom, she's only sixteen!"

178

My oldest brother Santos and I didn't need any such *dichos*.
I was too young, and Santos was the responsible one, quiet and
focused at working his way through college. However, every time
Mama Tere would see me engrossed in yet another book or my
brother Santos tinkering with his dead old car, she would shake her
head, laugh, and say, "*Cada chango con su mecate*. Every monkey
with their rope."

After early Sunday mass, we would come home and Mexican
charolas made of glazed brown clay would appear on our gas stove.
We immediately knew we were having *mole*, an ancient dish that my
mother and grandmother prepared from scratch that was finger licking
delicious. When we were gathered around our dining room table and
one of us got up to fetch something, someone would shout, "*El que
se fue pa' Torreón, perdió su sillón*," as they took the seat. And I would
follow with a *dicho* I made up, "*El que fue por sandia, perdió su silla*."

Because my sister Janie wore her emotions on her sleeves and
on her face, Mama Ruben would remind her, "*A mal tiempo, buena
cara* or when times are bad, put on a happy face." Also, "*Juanita, No
hay rosas sin espinas*. All roses have thorns."

Dichos spoke of love or life in general. Some are humorous
and others are blistering hot. Some offer advice and some are
brutally honest. We heard so many, some we remembered, but
many were forgotten.

Mama Ruben did not believe in long drawn-out lectures. She
said she could see our eyes glaze over and our minds wander. So, she
tried *dichos*, like the ones she grew up hearing, hoping some would
stick, and some did. To this day, I can recall many of the *dichos*
whirling in the air, aimed to keep us on the straight and narrow. I'd
been raised a good girl; I would soon learn I was the best of the best.

JOURNEY DOWN MEMORY LANE

I often pondered if people who didn't grow up in my neighborhood would find themselves in my stories. Also, I wondered about any similarities and differences that may link our human experiences regardless of place, time, culture, and language. My aim is that these recollections inspire readers to speak about and write their stories. To find out what we understand about ourselves and each other and what we have in common. As we honor the past and document our cultural traditions, we record ancestral legacies that would otherwise remain buried, and lost for eternity.

To each one who finds themselves in this narrative, I extend my appreciation. To those who've been in my life and walked a parallel path, thank you for the wisdom you imparted, intentionally or otherwise. As for our beloved Westside, often derided for its poverty and segregated as devalued, the foundation it provided gave me a rich and complete life.

Write. Write. Write. Document the legacies you carry. With our unearthed stories, we impart knowledge. If our stories aren't recorded and voiced, our memories will fade into nothingness. Share your *cuentos* with the world.

MAMA RUBEN, PAPA MUNDO, AND TERESITA—LOVERS OF BOOKS

PHOTOGRAPHS PROVIDED BY:

Teresa Villareal Rodriguez

Teresa Villarreal Rodriguez shares a migration story between Mexico and the United States. On her paternal side, she is a proud first-generation Mexican American born in San Antonio, Texas. On her mother's side, Teresa, a ninth generation *Tejana*, traces her roots to 1718.

A product of San Antonio Independent School District schools, Teresa earned a business degree from Incarnate Word College. Her career of forty-four years was spent in service to her community—first as a social worker and later as a high school teacher in an inner-city school.

Villarreal Rodriguez continues to reside in her beloved San Antonio, surrounded by her two children, four grandchildren, *y un montón de parientes y buenos amigos*. She continues to write about her city and community.